THE FALL OF A BLACK ARMY OFFICER

Also by Charles M. Robinson III

Frontier Forts of Texas (Houston, 1986)
The Frontier World of Fort Griffin: The Life and Death of a
    Western Town (Spokane, 1992)
Bad Hand: A Biography of General Ranald S. Mackenzie (Austin,
    1993)
The Court-Martial of Lieutenant Henry Flipper (El Paso, 1994)
Shark of the Confederacy: The Story of the CSS Alabama
    (Annapolis, 1995)
A Good Year to Die: The Story of the Great Sioux War (New York,
    1995; Norman, 1996)
Hurricane of Fire: The Union Assault on Fort Fisher (Annapolis,
    1998)
The Indian Trial: The Complete Story of the Warren Wagon Train
    Massacre and the Fall of the Kiowa Nation (Spokane, 1997)
Santana: The Life and Death of a War Chief (Austin, 1998)
The Men Who Wear the Star: The Story of the Texas Rangers
    (New York, 2000)
General Crook and the Western Frontier (Norman, 2001)
The Plains Wars, 1757–1900 (New York, 2003)
(ed.) The Diaries of John Gregory Bourke. 3 vols. (Denton, Tex.,
    2003, 2005, 2007)
Texas and the Mexican War: A History and a Guide (Austin,
    2004)
Roadside History of Louisiana (Missoula, Mont., 2007)

THE FALL OF A
BLACK ARMY OFFICER
RACISM AND THE MYTH
OF HENRY O. FLIPPER

Charles M. Robinson III

University of Oklahoma Press : Norman

Library of Congress Cataloging-in-Publication Data

Robinson, Charles M., 1949–
  The fall of a black army officer : racism and the myth of Henry
O. Flipper / Charles M. Robinson, III.
      p. cm.
  Includes bibliographical references and index.
  ISBN 978-0-8061-3521-2 (hardcover : alk. paper) 1. Flipper,
Henry Ossian, 1856–1940—Trials, litigation, etc.   2. Trials
(Military offenses)—Texas—Fort Davis.   3. Courts-martial and
courts of inquiry—United States.   I. Title.
  KF7642.F58R633 2008
  355.1'334—dc22
  [B]
                                                    2007049603

The paper in this book meets the guidelines for permanence and
durability of the Committee on Production Guidelines for Book
Longevity of the Council on Library Resources, Inc. ∞

1 2 3 4 5 6 7 8 9 10

To Thomas D. Phillips,
who raised many of the questions,
and Mary Williams, who helped in my attempt
to find the answers

It seems a pity to spoil a good story with a fact.

—Oscar Wilde

Lieut. Flipper has been a very good and attentive officer but his carelessness in this transaction is inexcusable.

—Colonel William R. Shafter, First U.S. Infantry

I declare to you in the most solemn and impressive manner possible that I am perfectly innocent in every manner, shape or form.

—Second Lieutenant Henry O. Flipper,
Tenth U.S. Cavalry

CONTENTS

ILLUSTRATIONS

PREFACE

This is not a history of institutionalized racism in the nineteenth-century military. It is the story of the trial and dismissal of one officer. Racism becomes an issue, however, in that the officer in question was black, and in how the case was handled, how it was perceived in his time, and more important, how it came to be seen more than eight decades later. Second Lieutenant Henry Ossian Flipper's race certainly was mentioned, both in the preliminaries to the trial and in the trial itself. Was race a key issue in his conviction and dismissal, or did it become a key issue only to fit the political and social agenda of a later era? That is the question this book attempts to address.

This project began as a revised edition of my book *The Court-Martial of Lieutenant Henry Flipper*, released by Texas Western Press, the publishing house of what is now the University of Texas at El Paso, in 1994. That book was the result of about ten years of research into the Flipper affair, and writing it led to substantial changes in my original view of the case. When I began, I firmly believed that Henry O. Flipper had been unjustly convicted on trumped-up charges because he was black, and after preliminary research, I was naïve enough to say so in a magazine article.[1] Like most people who have written on the Flipper affair, I relied on Flipper's 1898 petition for reinstatement, which contained enough extracts of court-martial transcripts and other records to seem credible. I had not yet examined the 600-plus-page transcript itself, nor the hundreds of pages of evidence and documentation. But even without a thorough examination of the entire record, Flipper's position was open to question. My original aim was to prove his case definitively through careful study of the full record of the court-martial.

Ultimately I did acquire a microfilm copy of the entire file.[2] But as I studied it, I came to the unpleasant realization that I had been wrong. Flipper, it now seemed to me, was the author of his own problems. I was not alone in this conclusion. In 1980 Barry C. Johnson published a monograph in England entitled *Flipper's Dismissal*, based on a thorough study of the trial and evidence, in which he also concluded that Flipper's own actions led to the charges against him.[3] Johnson had approached the subject with an open mind. As he later wrote to me, "I undertook the work, in the first place, because (though this sounds a bit pretentious) I was genuinely interested, intellectually, in trying to decide whether Lt. F. *was* a 'scapegoat' done down by wicked white prejudice."[4]

The Court-Martial of Lieutenant Henry Flipper was published as part of Texas Western Press's Southwestern Studies series, and as such it had to fit the format of that series. Consequently, portions of the book had to be cut to fit the requisite length, and some of the information was thus sketchy. Even so, the book generally was well received, although some reviewers noted the gaps in information left by the cuts. Meanwhile, the Flipper affair, which already had taken on a life of its own before I became involved, continued to unfold.

During the 1990s, a plethora of new material came out, especially as the Flipper advocates lobbied to memorialize him.

With the passage of time, I acquired substantial additional information on the Flipper affair. When *The Court-Martial of Lieutenant Henry Flipper* went out of print, and the rights reverted to me, I contracted with the University of Oklahoma Press for a revised edition with the new material. The completed manuscript was sent to several readers, including James N. Leiker, Johnson County Community College, Overland Park, Kansas, and author of *Racial Borders: Black Soldiers along the Rio Grande*. Jim Leiker caught something that I had missed—there was so much new material, and the conclusions on the extent of Flipper's culpability had changed so much that it had become an entirely different book, even warranting a new title. He made substantial and useful recommendations on how to round it out, and this work is the result.

The conclusions in this book—which are entirely my own—likely will change nothing. Over the past thirty years a whole body of mythology has grown up around the Flipper affair, and the mythology has received official sanction from the federal government. Flipper's many adherents will no more question the myth of his victimization than the devotees of St. Christopher will question the myth of a giant bearing the infant Christ across a river.

In some ways, the Flipper myth bears a resemblance to the myth of Dr. Charles R. Drew in the mid-twentieth century—a falsehood that reveals an ugly underlying truth. Dr. Drew, a noted black scientist and surgeon who pioneered blood plasma research, died of injuries sustained in an automobile accident in North Carolina in 1950. Within a day, rumors were flying that Drew bled to death because he had been refused transfusions at a whites-only hospital. Although the rumors are false (two white surgeons in a segregated hospital worked frantically to save his life), they point up the nineteenth-century army, referenced the appropriate army regulations, and suggested many different possible scenarios for the unanswered questions of the Flipper affair. Mary Williams, historian at Fort Davis National Historic Site, tolerated vague requests, repeated questions, unannounced visits, cancellations, and various and sundry annoyances, always with her characteristic good humor. Without her dedication above and beyond the call, many projects besides my own would never come to fruition. Special thanks also go to James N. Leiker for steering me in the right direction.

I am grateful as well to Maj. Benjamin M. Yudesis, USA (ret.), for background information on military justice and the system for courts-martial in the nineteenth century; to Barry C. Johnson, of Birmingham, England, for permission to quote from his book, *Flipper's Dismissal*, and for his overall encouragement on the original project; and to Dale L. Walker of El Paso, Texas, for his suggestions and encouragement on the original edition.

I wish to acknowledge the help and encouragement of Charles E. Rankin, Jean Hurtado, Greta Mohon, JoAnn Reece, and Daniel Simon of the University of Oklahoma Press.

The Booker T. Washington letters quoted here, and published by the University of Illinois Press, are in the Booker T. Washington Papers in the Library of Congress.

Portions of this book were drawn from *The Court-Martial of Lieutenant Henry Flipper*, copyright 1994 by Charles M. Robinson III, and published by Texas Western Press, University of Texas at El Paso.

THE FALL OF A BLACK ARMY OFFICER

Introduction

RACISM OR SELF-DESTRUCTION?

On September 17, 1881, a young army officer faced court-martial on the isolated frontier post of Fort Davis, Texas. That, in itself, was nothing unusual. Courts-martial were common in those days, there being few alternative forms of judgment in the army. Many an officer stood before a board on charges ranging from minor infractions to criminal offenses. In this trial, however, the difference was that the defendant was black. In fact, he was the only African American officer in the U.S. Army.

The court-martial of Second Lieutenant Henry Ossian Flipper, Tenth United States Cavalry, was not simply the trial of a soldier. To some degree, the army itself was on trial. In convicting Flipper and dismissing him from the service, the court-martial created a controversy that, even after more than a century, stirs heated debate.

A peculiar set of circumstances combined with his own personality to make Flipper a symbol of the legal and social upheavals of his day. Although he grew up a slave, he received opportunities denied even to many free white children of the period. As a cadet at West Point, he learned from the experiences of others and was successful. As an officer, he became arrogant and, if his own account is to be believed, deliberately courted disaster by flaunting the long-established, if unjust, codes of social behavior. In the mid-twentieth century, Flipper might have helped break the color barriers and bring about change. But he lived in an age when the color of his skin, combined with his own poor judgment, could blot out any previous achievement. Because of that, the Flipper affair has become so tangled in political and social agendas that the legal aspects have been obscured. Flipper himself tried to blame his fall on race, and the possibility that racism was behind the charges was mentioned during the trial. In the end, however, the issue was allowed to lapse in the face of the evidence. The Eastern black press initially took some note of Flipper's case but, in the end, proved to be only marginally interested in a court-martial on the remote frontier. The black leader Booker T. Washington, whom Flipper approached more than two decades later, likewise appears to have seen little in the case to warrant his attention. One therefore may conclude that Flipper's case truly became a racial issue only when it was resurrected in the 1960s, a time in which the so-called race card became the wild card that could tilt a hand.

There is no question that racism existed in the army. Between 1870 (the first year any black man was allowed the privilege) and 1889, only twenty-two African Americans were appointed to West Point, of whom twelve passed the entrance examinations. Of those twelve, only three graduated: Flipper in 1877, John H. Alexander in 1887, and Charles Young in 1889, all of whom faced harassment and disdain. After Young, no more black men would graduate until 1936. During this same period, in fact for thirty-two years from 1866 to 1898, not one black enlisted man rose from the ranks

The military world of Henry Flipper.

to receive an officer's commission, although it was not prohibited by Army Regulations.[1]

Despite this climate of unofficial discrimination, one cannot read the 606 pages of transcript to the Flipper court-martial
without coming to admire the members of the board for their
conduct of the trial. Every opportunity was given to Flipper to
present his defense. Indeed, in their effort to determine the
truth, and in keeping with the custom of the times in trying a
fellow officer, the court granted defense counsel Capt. Merritt
Barber substantial leeway in representing his client. While
upholding the right of Brig. Gen. Christopher C. Augur, commander of the Department of Texas, to appoint additional

members, the board nevertheless sustained Flipper's objections to those members. From there, the trial continued to lean slightly toward Flipper, with one member even inviting him to prove persecution as a factor in the initial charges.

Yet this remarkable record has been little used in investigating the Flipper affair. Going back over the various writings, the majority seem to have based their conclusions on Flipper's unsubstantiated allegations of persecution, and as Brig. Gen. Marcos E. Kinevan, professor emeritus of law at the United States Air Force Academy, has pointed out, with "little understanding of criminal or military law."[2] Until the publication of Barry Johnson's *Flipper's Dismissal* in 1980, few authors appear to have seriously considered the official record of the trial, or the extensive documentation that was used as evidence in the case. They have taken Flipper's word that he was the victim of a conspiracy, and that the good civilians of the Fort Davis business community warned him about a conspiracy. Yet, when those same civilians testified at the trial, they did so as character witnesses and made no mention of any conspiracy. Likewise, Flipper's word is contradicted by voluminous evidence.

In *The March of Folly*, Barbara W. Tuchman wrote, "The gods' interference does not acquit man of folly; rather, it is man's device for transferring the responsibility for folly."[3] Tuchman was referring to accounts of the Trojan War that attributed the sack of Troy and the tragedies that befell the victors to the capriciousness of the gods, rather than the actions of the Achaeans and Trojans themselves. Nevertheless, the same principle applies to modern times, where conspiracy becomes "man's device for transferring the responsibility for folly." Indeed, writers, film directors, politicians, evangelists, and professional activists have built lucrative careers on the idea of conspiracy. Whether political, criminal, social, racial, or demonic, a conspiracy provides some degree of comfort; it helps rationalize the irrational and explain the unexplainable. It also allows us to justify our failings and avoid responsibility for whatever we might have done to our own detriment. Such was the case when Flipper entered his petitions and wrote his later memoirs. Thus, he himself helped initiate the myth of the "railroaded Buffalo Soldier" that came to fruition in the social consciousness of the late twentieth century.

The questions, then, must be raised: was Flipper in fact a victim of racism in the sentence of dismissal? Or was he simply the victim of an arbitrary system of military justice (that continues even to the present), whereby the final disposition of a case rests on the whims of a high-level reviewing authority and an ephemeral "good of the service"?

The petition for pardon states, "Examination of the cases of white officers tried on similar or more serious charges demonstrates that had Lt. Flipper been white, *he almost certainly would not have been convicted* and would not have been dismissed from the Army [italics in original]."[4] The notion that he would not have been convicted is patently absurd. It was established beyond any doubt that he had issued a fraudulent check in excess of fourteen hundred dollars (a felony in itself), had misrepresented the accounts to his commanding officer, had repeatedly lied to his commanding officer, and had sent false reports to departmental headquarters in San Antonio. What second lieutenant would get away with that, even now? Common sense dictates that some sort of offense had been committed and that a guilty verdict would be returned upon trial, regardless of the race of the defendant.

Even the punishment has been distorted over time. Despite continuing allegations to the contrary, Flipper was *not* dishonorably discharged; he was dismissed. In dismissing him without comment, the War Department simply was saying that his services as a soldier were neither needed nor desired. In modern parlance, this would equate to a general discharge. Although the circumstances were not considered honorable, neither were they dishonorable. Though stigmatized by dismissal, and suffering the loss of any future in the military, Flipper nevertheless was free to reenter government service in some other capacity, as he subsequently did with success.[5]

A comparison to the case of Flipper's contemporary Johnson Whittaker is instructive, because they both involved guilty verdicts against African Americans: in Flipper's case, an officer, and in Whittaker's, an officer cadet.[6] Whittaker, who was likewise convicted of conduct unbecoming an officer and a gentleman, as well as conduct prejudicial to good order and discipline, initially had been sentenced to dishonorable discharge from West Point, a one-dollar fine, and one year imprisonment at hard labor. After returning the verdict, however, six members of the court-martial board signed a recommendation that the fine and imprisonment be mitigated, citing his "youth and inexperience." Among those signing was the president of the court, Brig. Gen. Nelson A. Miles, normally regarded as a hard-nosed, unforgiving martinet. A seventh member, the same Merritt Barber who later served as Flipper's defense counsel, submitted a separate recommendation for clemency, citing Whittaker's "youth[,] inexperience and the peculiar circumstances surrounding the case as shown by the testimony."[7] Only two of the board's nine members refrained from any recommendation. In Flipper's case, however, no one directly connected with the trial submitted a recommendation either for mitigated sentence or for clemency.

Two questions remain. First, was Flipper alone culpable? Second, was the sentence fair? When it comes to culpability, the army's own system of fiscal responsibility must carry some of the blame. As Lt. Col. Thomas T. Smith has pointed out in his study of the military impact on the nineteenth-century Texas economy, there were many instances in which an untrained junior officer was placed in charge of government funds, and then held liable for irregularities.[8] Colonel William R. Shafter, commanding officer at Fort Davis, must also share the blame for his cursory examination of the books, a symptom of his overall sloppy administration of the post. In modern times, it generally is impractical for a post commander to personally examine and verify the accounts. The commissary department has a myriad of clerks, and there is an extensive bureaucracy to conduct in-house examinations. In the nineteenth century, however, the duties of a post commander were much more extensive; the bureaucracy consisted of Flipper, one sergeant-clerk, one adjutant, and Shafter. In any case, a commander is responsible for actions of his subordinates.

Yet neither was Flipper as absolutely helpless as he attempted to make himself appear. Certainly nineteenth-century West Point, essentially an engineering school emphasizing the practical sciences with a smattering of liberal arts, was a poor training ground for quartermasters, paymasters, or commissary officers. These men learned their trade on the job. Even so, Flipper basically was dealing with printed forms, where he need only insert the proper amounts and total them up.[9] He had an experienced commissary clerk, Sgt. Carl Ross, to help him, and any number of other officers on post from whom he could get advice. If he was, in fact, ostracized by fellow officers at Fort Davis (another of his claims that is unsubstantiated by the evidence), he could have sought help from his businessmen friends in town.

While black leaders of today might hold up Flipper as a role model for his attainment as the first black graduate of the U.S. Military Academy, the indifference of those in his own time toward his troubles is easy to understand. He was the one black cadet who had come through four years of abuse at West Point to gain a commission as an army officer. Then, he was brought up on charges. Guilty or not, this essentially was a slap in the face to any African American who might hope for equality in the military, particularly as it came hard on the heels of the Whittaker affair. It is small wonder that the black community expressed little interest in his defense.

There is no question that the supposed villain of the scenario, Colonel Shafter, was determined to destroy Flipper, and with good reason. Flipper had submitted falsified financial reports, which Shafter had signed in good faith. When the reports were determined to be spurious, Shafter, at the very least, looked like a fool to his superiors in San Antonio. Then, as the investigation was under way, a letter appeared in the *Globe*, a black newspaper in New York, in which Flipper accused the colonel of conspiracy.[10] Shafter had made a career of handling black troops. Undoubtedly, during his thirteen years as lieutenant colonel of black Regulars, from 1866 until 1879, he had suffered the disdain that fellow white officers reserved for leaders of such troops. Nevertheless, during his tenure with the Twenty-fourth Infantry, he had molded it into a regiment with a proud record. Then came Flipper to cast a pall on black soldiers, and to seemingly undo everything Shafter and others like him had done. His outrage is understandable.

Because of the great social upheavals of the second half of the twentieth century, the Flipper affair has assumed a political and social significance that is entirely out of proportion to the historical reality. Although the case had been resolved decades earlier, it had to be re-resolved, regardless of the facts. For his family, this is understandable. For politicians and social activists, it is an imperative. The efforts culminated with a pardon issued to Flipper by President William J. Clinton on February 19, 1999. Clinton's speech at the pardoning ceremony was standard political fare. He perpetuated the myth of a dishonorable discharge and said, "Today's ceremony is about a moment in 1882, when our government did not do all it could do to protect an individual American's freedom. It is about a moment in 1999 when we correct the error and resolve to do even better in the future." He added that a "later

Army review board suggested he had been singled out for his race" but did not mention that this army review board convened more than ninety years after the fact, nor that its suggestions (as opposed to conclusions) were not unanimous.[11]

The political and legal machinations involved in the Flipper pardon, which take up over a thousand pages of briefs and petitions, are beyond the scope of this work. In view of his subsequent achievements, a pardon for an offense committed as a young man is entirely appropriate. Nevertheless, it must be remembered that a pardon is not an exoneration. The very use of the word "pardon" establishes that an offense was committed for which the government extends forgiveness. The record is not expunged. In the case of a living person, even after a presidential pardon has been issued, the recipient is still required to list the conviction whenever called upon to provide a criminal record.

In *The Black Regulars*, William A. Dobak and Thomas D. Phillips devote an entire chapter to military justice as applied to African American troops. Their conclusion is that there was little significant difference between the treatment of black enlisted men and their white counterparts by military courts, either in the conduct of their trials or in their sentences. Both were subjected to a system in which the needs of the army as an institution often took priority over justice.[12] Because the Flipper case involved an officer, however, no comparisons can be drawn concerning the overall treatment of black officers as opposed to white officers.

Nevertheless, injustices against black soldiers did occur, and the attention surrounding the Flipper affair and its questionable circumstances has overshadowed very real cases of racism in the military. These include the case of Johnson Whittaker at West Point, the so-called mutiny at Fort Stockton, Texas, and prejudicial treatment of black troops during the first half of the twentieth century. It is not the purpose of this book to discuss all the indignities inflicted on African Americans in the military. Nevertheless, Fort Stockton, like Whittaker, is worthy of mention because it occurred in the same era as Flipper, but has been more or less lost in the shuffle.

The Fort Stockton case began in April 1873, when Pvt. John Taylor, Twenty-fifth Infantry, a black regiment, reported sick. The surgeon, Dr. J. A. Cleary, treated him but did not excuse him from duty. He reported a second time and again was not excused; and the third time, July 6, he was confined overnight in the guardhouse for malingering and sent back to work the next morning. By midmorning, he was too sick to work and was taken to the hospital. Neither Cleary nor another surgeon passing through Stockton en route to his own assignment could determine the cause of the illness, but by noon Taylor was dead. According to Maj. Zenas Bliss, Twenty-fifth Infantry, who presided over the subsequent court-martial board, an autopsy showed an enlarged spleen, but no other irregularities.

Meanwhile, the troops began grumbling, and threats supposedly were made against Dr. Cleary. On July 14 the post commander, Capt. F. S. Dodge, Ninth Cavalry, received a "round robin" letter signed by the majority of the enlisted men accusing Cleary of intentional neglect in Taylor's death. When no action was taken, the troops became defiant, and sixty-two soldiers and noncommissioned officers were court-martialed en masse on August 26. All were found guilty and received sentences ranging from five to fifteen years. Case closed.[13]

In researching his landmark study of black soldiers on the frontier, Dr. William H. Leckie encountered no instances of white officers who met the same fate as Flipper for similar offenses, although a substantial number of officers were suspended.[14] One case raised by Barber during Flipper's trial concerned a paymaster named Reese, who was convicted of embezzlement through fraud and suspended for four months. Yet, as Barber himself noted, Reese had a far longer service record than Flipper. Nineteenth-century U.S. military justice, with its origins in Baroque Europe, emphasized the honor of the officer corps, and welfare of the army as an institution, rather than technicalities of law. A good service record often was a mitigating circumstance during that era, particularly if it included honorable service in the Union army during the Civil War. That was the defining moment of the nineteenth-century U.S. Army, and officers with distinguished records in the Union army were considered to be a cut above all others. Even when a court-martial did follow regulations and dismiss an officer, there was no guarantee that the dismissal would be upheld once it reached the civilian arm of government. This consisted of the president and secretary of war, almost invariably veterans, with interested congressmen watching from the side, many of whom also were veterans.[15] As such, they formed a brotherhood, careful to look after their own and protect them from the full weight of postwar army discipline. Frequently the military arm would sentence a veteran to dismissal, only to be overruled in favor of a lesser sentence by the political arm, generally to the resentment of the military.[16]

The only paymaster named Reese listed in Heitman's *Historical Register and Dictionary of the United States Army* is Maj. Henry Bickham Reese, who joined the Union army as a volunteer paymaster in 1861, and was breveted to lieutenant colonel of Volunteers in 1865 for "fai[ithful] and mer[itorious] ser[vice] during the war." Reese retired in 1888 and died in 1902. One must assume, then, that this is the Reese whom Barber meant.[17]

One must also consider an even more telling case, involving no less than Judge Adv. Gen. David G. Swaim, one of the senior reviewing officers of Flipper's conviction, who recommended Flipper's sentence of dismissal be mitigated. Within three years of the Flipper affair, Swaim himself was convicted of theft, the first serving judge advocate general to be tried by court-martial. He was reduced three grades to major and suspended for twelve years, which allowed him to reenter the army just in time to retire.[18] Here again, a service record undoubtedly was considered. During the Civil War, Swaim had been breveted to lieutenant colonel and colonel of Volunteers, for faithful and meritorious service, and to first lieutenant, captain, and major of the Regular Army, for "gal[lant] and mer ser dur[ing] the war."[19] Postwar officers, however, might not get off so easily. Indeed, Flipper was one of five officers sentenced by court-martial to dismissal in 1881, for making false statements and/or mishandling of funds.[20]

There is no question that Flipper's brief service in the army was good, a fact noted by the Army Board of Corrections in 1976. However, it is no more remarkable than those of many other junior officers who served in the Southwest during the Apache wars. In the final analysis, Flipper was dismissed for an offense committed as a soldier in a severe breach of discipline, veracity, and honor, in clear-cut violation of the Articles of War. In reviewing the facts of the case, the pardon is appropriate, but the upgrading of his discharge and the posthumous honors given him during the past decade must be seen as overcompensation to one man for the injustices done to an entire race. But it really doesn't matter. Lieutenant Henry O. Flipper is no longer a person; he is a symbol.

1

RACE AND THE ARMY

African Americans had served in various capacities outside the formal military structure since the Revolutionary War. The enlistment of black soldiers or militia, however,
was discouraged by slaveholders, who feared it might encourage insurrection. Ironically, with the outbreak of the Civil
War, the idea of enlisting black soldiers first gained currency
in the South, when individual Confederate states began
recruiting volunteer units of free African Americans even
before the first Battle of Manassas (Bull Run).[1] One such unit,
the Louisiana Colored Troops, even went so far as to have
black commissioned officers.[2] On a national level, though, no
such effort was made. Black men served as laborers and trans-
porters in the Confederate government forces, not as soldiers.
When the war continued with no end in sight, the army began
pressing for enlistment of black regular troops. The general
government resisted, its leaders arguing that a nationwide
recruitment of African Americans would lead to emancipation, which in turn would bring the end of the very society

the Confederacy was established to protect. But by February 1865 military realities forced the government to advocate formation of black regiments in exchange for emancipation. It was too late; the war was nearly over and black regular units were never organized.[3]

In the North, enlistment of African Americans into the United States Army was dictated by both altruism and military necessity. Concerned with maintaining the loyalty, or at least the neutrality, of slaveholding border states that had remained in the Union, Abraham Lincoln and his advisers initially took pains to establish that slavery was not an issue, and abolition not an objective of the war. For that reason, the government flatly opposed formation of black military units and even encouraged the return of fugitive slaves to their owners.[4]

Lincoln's position infuriated abolitionists, as well as prominent black leaders such as Frederick Douglass. Douglass demanded not only emancipation but the formation of regiments of African Americans, which would allow them to fight for their freedom. The western states refused to observe the government's order to return fugitive slaves. Some states offered black units to the federal government, which rejected them. Although Secretary of War Simon Cameron supported the use of black troops, the corruption and inefficiency in his department forced him from office before his views could have any effect.[5]

As the war dragged on, the progression of Union defeats or stalemates boosted the position of congressional Radicals who supported abolition. In March 1862 the military was forbidden to return fugitive slaves. More antislavery legislation was passed, gaining popular support until, by mid-1862, emancipation was an issue. In July Congress gave Lincoln discretionary power to enlist black soldiers.[6] The president, though, was not ready to employ them as combat troops, preferring instead to use them, as the Confederacy did, as laborers. This brought mixed reactions. Some thought it was beneath the dignity of the federal government to accept black help in winning the war. Others who recognized the political tightrope on which Lincoln was perched accepted the decision. For the abolitionists, however, it wasn't good enough, and papers such as the *Chicago Tribune* attacked the president for not using "every loyal arm," including black ones, to win the war.[7]

The decision already was being taken away from the government by some Union officers who were forming black units on their own and without authority. This development was brought on by purely military considerations. As more of the South was occupied, the army found itself with a large population of newly freed slaves. Some generals considered it good policy to withdraw them from the region, fearing they might again change hands and serve the Confederacy. Others argued they might be armed and turned against the South. By the end of the first full year of fighting, Union leaders knew that the war was far from over and that many more Federal soldiers would die. If a portion of the army consisted of black troops, the chance of losing an equivalent number of whites was diminished. Aggravating the problem was the fact that, by mid-1862, the early tide of patriotic enthusiasm had ebbed, and the number of white volunteers had dwindled to a trickle. This prompted generals to act on their own, enlisting black men to fill the gaps.[8]

One of those acting on his own was Maj. Gen. David Hunter, who in May 1862 ordered the enlistment of former slaves in occupied areas of South Carolina, Georgia, and Florida. Because of government resistance, the regiment was not formally mustered until January of the following year. By then the first official Federal black regiment, the Louisiana Native Guards, had been mustered in occupied New Orleans on September 27, 1862, at the instigation of Maj. Gen. Benjamin F. Butler.[9]

The Union had an even harder time instituting a black officer corps. Butler had tried to use black officers in his Native Guards but had discontinued the practice because of conflicts with white officers. It generally was understood throughout the Union army that black soldiers would be limited to enlisted and noncommissioned ranks, while officers would be white.[10] Nevertheless, about seventy-five black commissioned officers ultimately served, with even more serving as line officers, which is to say, combat appointments.[11]

Despite political and social opposition to their service, black soldiers were an unqualified success, distinguishing themselves in combat from the Atlantic Ocean to the Indian Territory. For those who had been slaves, military service provided an opportunity to show they were human beings and not property. The war also bridged the racial gap—for the duration at least—between blacks and whites. The stated Confederate policy was that white officers captured while commanding black troops would be executed for inciting servile insurrection, and black prisoners would be remanded to slavery. Surrender not being an option in black units, officers and men depended heavily on each other. In reality, the Confederate military tended to observe the policy in the breach, often treating captives as prisoners of war. Nevertheless, the prospect that officers could be executed, and rank and file returned to slavery, created new respect for black troops among their white Union counterparts. Attacks on the war itself by the Northern peace faction likewise forced white soldiers, who believed in the war's aims, to defend black enlistment as a means of achieving victory.[12]

By July 1865, three months after the end of the war, the United States Army had 123,156 black soldiers in the infantry, cavalry, light artillery, and heavy artillery. The number was diminished, however, by the rapid demobilization of the armed forces, to such an extent that the number of active military personnel reached an alarmingly low level, particularly in view of conditions on the frontiers.[13] In the West, American Indian groups had taken advantage of the wartime withdrawal of troops to initiate a series of devastating depredations. In Mexico, Benito Juárez's Republican Reformists were in a life-or-death struggle with Maximilian's Imperialists and conditions on that border were chaotic. More troops were needed, and many who had been mustered out at war's end, before their terms were completed, were recalled to active duty. These included African Americans, some of whom had signed three-year enlistments as late as 1864.[14]

On July 28, 1866, as part of the postwar reorganization of the army, Congress authorized six new black regiments, two of cavalry and four of infantry.[15] The following month, U. S. Grant, commanding general of the army, ordered the organization of the two cavalry regiments, which were numbered the Ninth and Tenth. Command of the Tenth was given to Col. Benjamin Grierson, a former music teacher who had a brilliant career as a Union cavalry officer.[16] Tough but humane, Grierson was fiercely protective of his troops. To him, they were simply soldiers and, although the unit was officially designated "Tenth Regiment of Cavalry (Colored)," he refused to allow the word "colored" in company reports.[17]

Not everyone was impressed. Captain William George Wedemeyer, Sixteenth Infantry, who had known Grierson at Fort Concho, Texas, commented, "I don't admire Gen. Grierson's ways. He is a great talker and full of himself and his works." Another soldier of the Sixteenth, Cpl. Emil A. Bode, who, like Wedemeyer, was a German, described Grierson as an officer "who preferred the safe side."[18]

Whatever his flaws, Grierson was admirable for not sharing the general aversion to service with black troops that prevailed among white officers after the war. Many officers tended to avoid assignment to black regiments, even going so far as to accept lower rank in white units. Part of the problem was personal prejudice, but part also was the general atmosphere surrounding the black regiments. Whereas officers of U.S. Colored Troops during the war frequently were old-line professionals for whom the threat of a Confederate gallows was simply another risk of war, officers of newly organized postwar black regiments often were viewed as too incompetent to command white soldiers and could expect assignment to the more remote regions of the country, away from any sort of social amenities.

Recent studies have disputed the common assumption that there was systematic official discrimination against black regular soldiers. They had the same legal protection as whites, generally were issued the same equipment, and were not prohibited by law or regulation from receiving commissions as officers. Nevertheless, the army was sensitive to local opinion. Many communities in the South resented the presence of any military garrison in the vicinity, but they particularly resented black soldiers. In Texas, black soldiers initially faced dual ostracism: they were resented as symbols of Reconstruction in a former Confederate state, and they were resented because they were black. By 1869 tensions were such that virtually all black troops were pulled out of the population centers and reassigned to remote posts of West Texas, such as Forts McKavett, Stockton, Davis, Quitman, Concho, and Griffin. Some of these posts predated the Civil War and had sat abandoned throughout the war and the years immediately following. They had to be completely reconstructed and in the cases of Davis and Stockton relocated to more suitable sites. Accommodations often were rudimentary. At Fort Davis, the scene of Flipper's court-martial, the first garrison of black troops found that their adobe barracks partially dissolved during heavy rains, dripping ooze down on them at meals. There was little air circulation, and men tended to be healthier on field duty than they were on post. The government justified its negligence on the premise that African Americans adapted more readily to the heat, ironically the same rationale used by antebellum Southern planters in justifying slavery.

Likewise, when problems arose with the local white civilian population, the government often acquiesced to community pressure, rather than consider the problems the African American soldiers may have faced. In his study of black troops along the Rio Grande, James N. Leiker has pointed to several altercations between soldiers and civilians in Laredo (Fort McIntosh), Brownsville (Fort Brown), and Rio Grande City (Fort Ringgold) in the nineteenth and early twentieth centuries. In such cases, popular feeling among the white citizens almost invariably prevailed. Nor did individual officers hesitate to express their own views that somehow black soldiers were less deserving than their white counterparts.[19]

One of the problems faced by commanders of black regiments was the quality of the soldiers. During the Civil War, officers had to give more attention to detail, overseeing everything from sanitary needs to minor paperwork—jobs that in white regiments generally were handled by sergeants and clerks. The frontier army was no different, having more than its share of uneducated former field hands. The government, meanwhile, set high standards for the officers in black outfits, and the officers, in turn, expected high standards of the troops. Dissatisfied with the abilities of newly emancipated slaves, they opened recruiting offices in the Northern states, in order to attract African Americans with a broader background. These efforts were only partly successful, and the problem remained, placing a greater burden on the officers. As one sergeant of a white cavalry regiment remarked: "The intimate and practical knowledge of the requirements of the men thus obtained, in addition to the greater responsibility thus placed on their shoulders, accounts for the marked efficiency I have noticed among [the officers of black units] as a class."[20]

In view of these circumstances, Henry Flipper's commission as an officer was, in itself, an anomaly. Although the legislation authorizing the black regiments did not address the issue of race, clear barriers of color remained; it was presumed officers would be white.[21] Occasionally, the barriers were justified by practical reasons. Brigadier General Edward O. C. Ord, whose postwar administrative commands included black troops, observed that the army did not attract an educated class. Most African Americans were former slaves, trained all their lives toward obedience. It was unreasonable, in his view, to assume they possessed the qualifications for command.[22]

Ord's attitude was shared by Maj. Gen. John M. Schofield, superintendent of the United States Military Academy, who complained in an annual report:

> To send to West Point for four years' completion a young man who was born in slavery is to assume that half a generation has been sufficient to raise a level which the average white man has reached in several hundred years. As well might the common farm horse be entered in a four-mile race against the best blood inherited from a long line of English racers.[23]

Ironically, Schofield made these remarks in 1880, three years after Henry Flipper had finished the race at West Point and had become a commissioned officer in the Tenth United States Cavalry.

2

The Black Cadet

Henry Ossian Flipper was born in Thomasville, Georgia, on March 21, 1856. He and his mother, Isabella Buck-halter, were the property of the Rev. Reuben H. Lucky, a Methodist minister. Henry's father, Festus Flipper, belonged to Ephraim G. Ponder, a prosperous slave trader.[1] Festus Flipper was trained as a shoemaker and carriage trimmer, and this put him in a relatively high position in the slave hierarchy. Skilled slaves did much of the specialty work, not only on the plantations, but in the Southern towns and cities as well. Indeed, a very large proportion of skilled labor in the South was the province of slaves or free African Americans. They were fully aware of their importance and took pride in their positions, which they jealously guarded against any challenge.[2] Many of Ponder's people were highly skilled, and their master allowed them to contract their free time. "Mr. Ponder would have absolutely nothing to do with their business other than to protect them," young Henry later recalled. "These bonded people were therefore virtually free. They acquired and accumulated wealth, lived happily, and needed but two other things to make them like other human beings, viz. Absolute freedom and education."[3] Even so, the Ponder arrangement ultimately allowed Festus to purchase his wife and children (for now there was a second son, Joseph) from Lucky. Given Henry's later attitudes toward life, there is little doubt that he was fully aware of his father's status in the slave community.

Fortune continued to favor the Flippers, who had relocated to Atlanta when Ponder married a woman there. The household was in domestic turmoil, and eventually Ponder left his wife and returned to Thomasville. Under the marriage contract, neither he nor his wife could sell anything without the other's consent, and Mrs. Ponder had little interest in the day-to-day activities of the slaves. Left to their own devices and free of any real interference, they continued to develop their business interests. One, John F. Quarles, had a basic education and obtained permission to open a night school in the wood shop even though it was in violation of Georgia law. Here, at the age of eight, Henry began learning to read, write, and cipher.[4]

As the Union army approached Atlanta, Mrs. Ponder and the slaves took refuge in Macon. Then, in the spring of 1865, Festus Flipper took his wife and sons back to the ruins of Atlanta, moving into one of the few houses that remained. Flipper's personal holdings were intact, and when compared to many whites in the city, the family was well-to-do. One of their neighbors, the widow of a Confederate officer, was hired to tutor the two boys. In March 1866 they transferred to one of the new schools opened by the American Missionary Association, and in 1869 they enrolled in the association's Atlanta University. The family, meanwhile, had two more sons, Carl and Festus, Jr.[5]

Although emancipation provided freedom from bondage, it aggravated existing problems among the newly freed slaves and created new ones. Slaves had developed a rigid hierarchy of caste that was strengthened by the existence of an affluent class of free African Americans (often of mixed blood), not only in the antebellum North but in the South as well. Among other things, the degree of color defined status. The lighter the skin, the higher the social standing, and the paler, generally urban "colored society" sniffed in contempt at dark-skinned "country blacks." Education was another factor; those who were educated, particularly along white lines, formed an elite. Finally, there was a segment of the African American population that attempted to emulate all the trappings of the whites, fashioning themselves into darker-skinned replicas of the dominant race.[6] Somewhere along the way, Henry Flipper appears to have acquired many of these traits. He was very conscious that he was pale, urban, and educated, and his subsequent writings and actions tended to denigrate those who were not, or who did not somehow fit into the replicated mold. The first indication came in the fall of 1872, when he overheard a conversation in his father's workshop about the cadet then representing the Flippers' congressional district at West Point. As that cadet would graduate the following June, there would be a vacancy, and he decided to apply.[7]

Reconstruction had effectively ended in Georgia two years before Flipper's appointment, and upon regaining control of the state in 1870, the Democrats began passing a series of laws designed to disenfranchise African Americans and remove them from the political scene.[8] Nevertheless, the effects of Reconstruction were still felt. It remained possible for a black candidate to be nominated to the academy, assuming a Republican was elected from that candidate's congressional district and the candidate showed himself to be worthy. When Republican J. C. Freeman was elected from the fifth district of Georgia, Flipper wrote to him, asking for a nomination. After obtaining endorsements from prominent local Republicans, Freeman advised him of the various entrance requirements. On April 21, 1873, Dr. Thomas Powell of Atlanta, the family physician, examined Flipper and certified him as meeting the academy's physical requirements. He also was examined for academic ability and declared proficient. Six days later, Freeman sent the nomination to the secretary of war, and on April 17, 1873, Flipper filled out a form acknowledging his candidacy.[9]

Five other black men were appointed as cadets before Flipper, but most either had been rejected or dismissed.[10] By the time he arrived on May 20, 1873, only James Webster Smith remained. Smith, the first to enter, had been introduced to discrimination upon arrival at West Point, where he had been refused a meal at the government-owned Rose Hotel.[11] Shunned and harassed at the academy, he began retaliating and soon gained a reputation as a troublemaker. Smith also took his case to a newspaper, an action that brought reprimands against some of the cadets who tormented him but alienated those on the academy staff who otherwise might have helped him.[12]

Experience had mellowed Smith to some extent by the time Flipper arrived, and he sent Flipper a letter warning him of pitfalls and how to avoid them. "It was a sad letter," Flipper remembered later. "I don't think anything has so affected me or so influenced my conduct at West Point as its melancholy tone."[13]

Flipper's first day likewise was unpleasant. As he walked from the adjutant's office to the barracks after checking in, he was jeered by some of the cadets standing at the windows. As the day passed, he began to theorize that he would have to face not only the basic prejudice of the white cadets but also the impression of African Americans as a whole created by Smith. This would not be the last time he would blame other black people for hindering his opportunities.

Impressions notwithstanding, Flipper and Smith became friends, and within a few days, they were joined by another black candidate, John Washington Williams. Flipper and Williams both did well on their preliminary examinations, but on the semiannual reexamination, six months later, Williams was found deficient. He was brought to Flipper for tutoring; despite that, he failed and was dismissed. Then, in June 1874, Smith failed one of his examinations and also was dismissed.[14]

Privately, Flipper tended to blame Smith and the other African Americans before him for their own downfalls. He was, in fact, an elitist, just as were the white cadets who considered themselves above the mainstream of white society.[15] In his memoir, *The Colored Cadet at West Point*, published in 1878, the year after graduation, Flipper attacked the notion that people automatically should be treated equally, stating that social equality was not an automatic right, but a privilege to be earned by education and character. Any attempt to legislate equality, he believed, was "unjust if not impolitic."

The idea that African Americans suffered discrimination based solely on skin color, Flipper maintained, was

one of which we should speedily rid ourselves. It may be color in some cases, but in the great majority of instances it is mental and moral condition. Little or no education, little moral refinement, and all their repulsive consequences will never be accepted as equals of education, intellectual or moral. Color is absolutely nothing in the consideration of the question, unless we mean by it not color of skin, but color of character.

Needless to say, he claimed social equality for himself, on a par with anyone else educated to become an army officer. "We have much in common," he wrote, "and this fact alone creates my right to social and equal recognition."[16]

In other words, Flipper was equal because he was "West Point." As for Smith and others, this was not necessarily the case. He also emphasized (in print) his own lighter complexion compared to several of the earlier black cadets. Except for his skin color Flipper was, as several historians have noted, a typical Southern aristocrat. This cavalier attitude earned Flipper the studied indifference of many leaders of the nation's black community, indifference that would manifest itself a few years later when he most needed their support.[17]

With Smith gone, Flipper found that white cadets who tried to be friendly soon were told by their peers to avoid him. Unlike Smith, he did not express his resentment and generally was left alone. Only when the abuse infringed on his class privileges did he make an issue of it, and in such cases, he was upheld. Aside from his loneliness over the next three years, his recollections of that period show his experiences to be similar to those of other cadets, and in some ways, perhaps more pleasant; as a social outcast he was spared much of the hazing and other harassments inflicted on plebes by upperclassmen. Gradually, his quiet dignity won the respect of the others.[18]

On August 23, 1876, another black cadet, Johnson Whittaker of South Carolina, arrived at West Point. Although, as the only African Americans at the academy, they roomed together, and Flipper was assigned to prepare Whittaker for his examinations, it is unlikely that Flipper allowed himself to become very close. The new cadet was three years his junior, and Flipper was always mindful of his class privileges. Their relationship appears to have been friendly, but formal. Flipper's influence, however, was obvious in Whittaker's conduct. Both disliked Smith's belligerent attitude, and Whittaker followed Flipper's example of ignoring minor insults while standing his ground when his rights were infringed upon.[19]

Like Flipper's, Whittaker's brief career became a symbol of the gulf separating black from white in military institutions of the time, and their cases would become intertwined. Whittaker, however, had far more grounds for complaint than Flipper. During the night of April 5–6, 1880, he was attacked in his room, bound, severely beaten, and cut. A court of inquiry, acting all too hastily and with too little examination of the evidence, determined that Whittaker had inflicted the injuries on himself to gain attention, discredit the academy, and avoid the June examinations. Whittaker then demanded a court-martial to clear his name. The court-martial found him guilty but disallowed the very basis of the government's position—the motive. The case dragged on until March 22, 1882, almost two years after Whittaker's ordeal began, when President Chester A. Arthur threw out the verdict on the grounds that a court-martial was not legally applicable in this situation. By then, however, the issue was moot: Whittaker had failed his exams, and Secretary of War Robert Todd Lincoln approved the academic board's recommendation for dismissal.

These troubles, however, were in the future when Henry Flipper graduated on June 14, 1877. As he marched up to receive his diploma, a cheer went up from his classmates. He finished fiftieth in a class of seventy-six, with a commission as a second lieutenant in the United States Army. Within a month, he had been appointed to Colonel Grierson's Tenth Cavalry, stationed on the Texas frontier.[20]

The assignment had some impact on his personal life. A year earlier, he had become engaged to Anna White, whom he had met as a student at Atlanta University. She broke the engagement, however, in part because her parents worried about the hardships of a frontier post, and in part because Joseph Flipper, now an ordained minister, feared his brother was not ready for marriage.[21]

The Tenth Cavalry was scattered in posts across the Texas plains and the Indian Territory. Flipper was ordered to join his unit, Company A, at Fort Concho, Texas, but on arrival in Houston, he learned that the company was en route to Fort Sill, Indian Territory. When he reached Sill, he was made post signal officer. The signal service was not the specialized branch that it is today and many of the duties—night signaling with torches, telegraphy, establishing and opening communications between two points—were part of the standard curriculum at West Point.[22] In addition to signaling, Flipper handled miscellaneous duties, including supervising and construction of a ditch to drain a boggy area on the post and temporarily commanding one of the other companies when all its officers were absent. He also began work on *The Colored Cadet at West Point*.[23]

This memoir, written while Flipper was young, just graduated, with his army career and life ahead of him, may be viewed as fairly reliable, at least insofar as his own experiences are concerned. A second memoir, *Negro Frontiersman*, is less so. Written in 1916 largely for the benefit of a "Mrs. Brown"—identified as an Augusta, Georgia, lady with whom he supposedly had a platonic friendship—*Negro Frontiersman* reads like a tainted self-justification, which, to a great degree, it is. By then, it had been established beyond any doubt that, whatever his good points, Flipper had lied to his commanding officer, been negligent with government funds, brought allegations against officers no longer alive to defend themselves, and contradicted himself on many points. So much of the memoir is contradicted by evidence that, at this late date, it is difficult to determine what is fact and what is fabrication. Consequently, readers must draw their own conclusions.[24]

Whatever his future might hold, however, Flipper's introduction to the army in the field was pleasant. The commander of Company A, Capt. Nicholas Nolan, was a tough professional soldier from Ireland and the regiment's most experienced Indian fighter.[25] Nolan considered Flipper "all that West Point turns out." He and his family received some criticism for receiving Flipper from "the lady of some officer, who, I presume, never smelt powder. . . . This, evidently, is done on account of his color and no allowance is made for his grand attainments."[26] He noted Flipper's relationship with the other officers in the company was cordial, and the more they came to know him, the more they considered him worthy of his position.[27]

Soon after the company's arrival at Fort Sill, Nolan, over fifty and a widower with two small children, went to San Antonio, where he married Annie Dwyer, the twenty-one-year-old daughter of former Bexar County Judge Thomas A. Dwyer. The new Mrs. Nolan joined her husband at Fort Sill, accompanied by her sister, Mollie Dwyer. This domestic situation was not unusual on the frontier, where unmarried female relatives would spend long visits that might even turn into more or less permanent arrangements. Nevertheless, it would become a key matter decades later, as Flipper looked for ways to justify his subsequent problems.[28]

Although Flipper at first moved carefully around the other officers, he gradually adopted the attitude of social equality. In fact, as the only black officer, he seems to have enjoyed a certain celebrity status. In one instance, Flipper's company was on an extended scout and, after four months in the field, went to Fort Concho to resupply. "We camped near the Post and there was a constant stream of colored women, soldiers' wives, etc., to see the colored officer," he recalled.

During that same encampment, an incident may have occurred that reminded Flipper he had no special position. One day Lt. Wallace Tear of the black Twenty-fifth Infantry came to camp to inform Flipper that the officers of Fort Concho were planning a dinner in his honor, giving him the time and date. The next day, however, Tear returned, apologized, and told Flipper that Maj. Anson Mills, commanding the post in Colonel Grierson's absence, had forbidden it, even though Mills was a member of Flipper's regiment. Since the other officers were still friendly, he appears to have written the incident off as a quirk in Mills's personality. In view of his later support for Flipper's reinstatement, it is possible that the thoroughly professional Mills simply objected to a dinner honoring a junior officer for no particular reason besides color (assuming, of course, that such dinner plans actually existed and were not a product of Flipper's vivid postarmy imagination).[29]

In the spring of 1880, Flipper's company, along with two companies from Fort Sill, were transferred first to Fort Elliott, in the Texas Panhandle, and then to Fort Davis, in the Trans-Pecos area of West Texas. The Warm Springs Apache chief Victorio had led an outbreak, and he now was terrorizing the southwestern United States and northern Mexico. Colonel Grierson moved his headquarters from Fort Concho to Fort Davis to organize a campaign in conjunction with his Mexican counterpart, Col. Joaquín Terrazas. Company A was sent to Fort Quitman, on the Rio Grande, where Nolan was advised that Victorio had raided a picket post downriver, killed several soldiers, and carried off most of their equipment and horses. Flipper was sent to inform Grierson, who was camped at Eagle Springs, ninety-eight miles away. He made the ride in twenty-two hours, after which Grierson threw back Victorio and drove him into Mexico, where he eventually was killed by Terrazas's forces. The following year, when Flipper desperately needed a friend, Grierson wrote a recommendation praising his character and "his efficiency and gallantry in the field," yet despite these accolades, he would not appear in court in Flipper's behalf.[30]

3

LINKS IN A CHAIN

Named for then–secretary of war Jefferson Davis, Fort Davis was established in 1854 to protect the road between San Antonio and El Paso. It was destroyed during the Civil War, so the post Flipper knew was a reconstruction begun in 1867, several hundred yards east of the original. There was a large parade ground, with enlisted barracks on the east side, officers' houses on the west, headquarters and post chapel on the north, and commissary and post trader on the south.[1] Except for the south side, where Sleeping Lion Mountain blocked expansion beyond the trader's building, the quadrangle was surrounded by support structures, such as hospital, stable, corrals, guardhouse, and quarters for servants and laundresses. The post commander had a house to himself. Other officers shared duplex quarters, divided down the center by a common hallway. The kitchens were detached structures to the rear.

At Fort Davis, Flipper was named acting assistant quartermaster and acting commissary of subsistence (ACS).

These positions made him responsible for "the entire military reservation, houses, water and fuel supply, transportation, feed, clothing and equipment for troops and the food supply."[2] He also was responsible for a great deal of money, because the Subsistence Department was legally empowered to sell goods from the post's stores to officers, enlisted men, and under certain conditions, civilians. Flipper received payment for subsistence goods and generally had more money on hand than was needed for the post. After closing the books each month, he was required to transfer surplus funds to the chief commissary officer of the Department of Texas in San Antonio, withholding one hundred dollars for contingencies. This transfer was to be made only when it could be done safely, by means of checks turned in by the officers. In addition, each ACS was required to send a weekly statement of funds to the chief commissary in San Antonio.[3]

Flipper always claimed his downfall began with a relationship with Captain Nolan's sister-in-law, Mollie Dwyer, which for that time was socially condemned. At Fort Sill, he said, he and Mollie "became fast friends and used to go horseback riding together."[4] They continued at Fort Davis, where she had moved as part of Nolan's household. In *Negro Frontiersman*, he attempted to convey that these rides were more than casual and hinted he may have been in love with her.

Such a relationship would have been extremely awkward in the context of the 1880s. As a group, white women in the West viewed African Americans with the same disdain as their Eastern sisters; the old prejudices simply moved along with them from one region to the other. Black people were considered inferior because of race, color, and their status as former slaves. Physical features, also, were used to parody them or to describe them simply as "hideous."[5] Even if Mollie Dwyer did not share these prejudices, as the daughter of a county judge whose duties would have included enforcing Texas's antimiscegenation laws, she would have been more than slightly aware of the awesome social and legal barrier between herself and Flipper.[6]

Given these circumstances, the supposedly intimate horseback-riding sessions involving a black army officer and a white woman should have stirred at least some comment. An isolated garrison like Fort Davis had few, if any, secrets. Yet aside from Flipper's 1916 memoir, there seem to be no letters or diary entries from anyone on the matter.[7] Flipper apparently fabricated the story to blame his downfall on rivalry over Mollie's affections between himself and Lt. Charles Nordstrom, Tenth Cavalry, his own company's first lieutenant. Nordstrom, Flipper said, "had no education and was a brute. He hated me and gradually won Miss Dwyer from her horse back rides with me and himself took her riding in a buggy he had."[8]

Even without the rivalry over Mollie, if indeed it existed, it is unlikely Flipper and Nordstrom got along. His description of Nordstrom as a "brute" is verifiable. On two previous occasions, he had been convicted by court-martial of abusing black soldiers, once for cursing a man in front of the entire company and once for beating a first sergeant with a club. The latter offense earned him a six-month suspension from rank and command, confinement to post, and forfeiture of seventy-five dollars a month from pay. Any contempt Flipper felt for him on that score would have been aggravated because Nordstrom essentially was a self-made soldier, who entered the army as a private in the First Maine Cavalry in 1862, and served in that capacity for the remainder of the Civil War. He received a second lieutenant's commission in 1867, likely because of his Union army background. Thus Flipper, who viewed uneducated or self-made people of any race as his social inferiors, would have had little use for Nordstrom regardless of circumstances. The problem was exacerbated because they shared duplex quarters connected by a common hall.[9]

As 1881 dawned, an event occurred that became the first link in the chain leading to Flipper's fall. On December 28,

1880, Charles Berger, a civilian scout employed by the army, applied to Nordstrom, then serving as post adjutant, for ten days' leave and a government horse to go to Fort Stockton. As Berger was an employee of long standing and thought to be of good character, permission was granted, and Flipper was authorized to furnish a horse.[10] Berger then disappeared with the horse as well as beef vouchers from the quartermaster's department, and on January 8, 1881, he was listed as a deserter. A board convened to look into the case determined that neither Flipper as quartermaster, nor Maj. N. B. McLaughlin, Tenth Cavalry, post commander, was responsible for Berger's actions or the missing property, and recommended that Flipper drop the horse from his returns.[11]

Flipper subsequently drew Berger's pay of sixty dollars for the entire month of January, reimbursed the post trader twenty dollars that Berger owed, and kept the balance as cash on hand. He reported these facts to both McLaughlin and his successor, Col. William R. Shafter, First Infantry. This innocuous financial arrangement would be used against Flipper later in the year.[12]

McLaughlin, an experienced soldier considered by Flipper to be "a fine officer and gentleman,"[13] was relieved by Colonel Shafter on March 12, 1881. Shafter, who also commanded the First Infantry, was a superb officer, whose operations against American Indians in the Pecos River area of West Texas had won him the nickname "Pecos Bill." He had commanded black troops during the Civil War. After the war, he was appointed lieutenant colonel of the black Forty-first Infantry, getting the position because the candidate initially appointed declined to serve with black soldiers. When the Forty-first was amalgamated with another African American unit to become the Twenty-fourth Infantry, Shafter continued as lieutenant colonel. Despite racist attitudes that he barely concealed, which were no different from those of mainstream white society of that era, he protected his troops.

On one occasion, in 1872, when he learned that soldiers assigned to guard stagecoach stations not only were denied transportation back to their posts when their duty ended but also denied food and shelter at the stations, he demanded that they receive both.[14] For all his irascibility, he had built the Twenty-fourth into a regiment that compared favorably with any unit, white or black, on the frontier. He served with the regiment until 1879, when promotion to colonel brought his transfer to the white First Infantry.

His record notwithstanding, Shafter was known as a martinet, who played favorites and harassed subordinates he disliked. A white corporal whose company was posted to Fort Davis at the time described Shafter as "a good and daring leader, but a man without morals or character." He essentially was a field soldier, and although he paid close attention to the men under his command, even to the point of personally conducting inspection, he had no particular interest in the routine, day-to-day administration of the post. The burden of commissary accounting fell totally on Flipper with no reliable reexamination, forging a second link in the chain to Flipper's fall.[15]

Incoming commanders often bring their own staffs, and Shafter was no exception. Besides his wife, the regimental band, and various other components of headquarters, he was accompanied by his adjutant, Lt. Louis Wilhelmi, and his quartermaster, Lt. Louis Harvie Strother.[16] Immediately upon assuming command, he issued orders relieving 2nd Lt. William C. McFarland, Sixteenth Infantry, as adjutant, and Flipper as quartermaster, replacing them with Wilhelmi and Strother, respectively. Flipper later contended Shafter informed him he also would be relieved as ACS as soon as a replacement could be found. Shafter never denied this, saying he felt Flipper, as a cavalry officer, would be more useful with his company in the field.[17] In later years, however, Flipper would make much of this, allowing the impression that he was the only man relieved of a position, and even claiming that Shafter, Nordstrom, and Wilhelmi "began to persecute me and lay traps for me. . . . [N]ever did a man walk the path of uprightness straighter than I did, but the trap was cunningly laid."[18]

Although Flipper said he expected to be relieved as ACS in "a few days," the days stretched into weeks. Then, on May 2, 1881, Maj. Michael P. Small, chief commissary of subsistence in San Antonio, notified all post commissary officers in the department that he would be absent from headquarters for the remainder of the month and that no funds were to be remitted to him until June. Meanwhile, Shafter continued to inspect the commissary funds and sign the weekly statements until May 28. After that, there was no inspection of funds, no weekly statements were submitted, and apparently no one inquired why.[19]

Without regular submissions to San Antonio, the commissary procedures at Fort Davis became haphazard, with no serious attempt by either Flipper or Shafter to ascertain that everything was in order. When Small extended his absence from headquarters into the latter part of June, Flipper found his department short on funds. He was not particularly concerned, because part of it was his own "considerable bill" yet unpaid (later testimony showed he owed $1,121.77 on his own account) and part, he knew, was owed by soldiers and laundresses and would be collected.[20]

On June 29, Small, now back in San Antonio, asked Flipper for all subsistence funds as of June 30, as soon as possible after closing his books for the month and deducting post expenses.[21] The letter arrived on July 8 by way of post headquarters, where Shafter saw it and ordered Flipper to submit his funds for inspection immediately. Flipper went to his quarters, where he kept the money in a trunk, and found himself still short, this time by a very substantial amount. Between two hundred and three hundred dollars were owed by officers on detached service or in the field, and since Shafter refused to inspect until all funds were in, Flipper borrowed that amount for the occasion. To cover the balance, he included a personal check for $1,440.43. Satisfied, Shafter told him to forward the funds to San Antonio. The following day, Flipper gave Shafter his weekly statement, which said, "In transit to . . . Dept. [of] Texas, San Antonio, Texas, $3,791.77." This was false; the available funds, still far short of the amount due, remained scattered haphazardly about his quarters.[22]

Flipper knew he could cover part of it by collecting from absent officers when they returned to post. The balance was another matter, since he did not have a bank account to cover his $1,440.43 check. He later contended he thought he was owed a large royalty payment on his autobiography and could only hope it would reach him in time to cover the check. Major Small again had left San Antonio for an inspection tour, and Flipper knew he would be gone until the end of July. Meanwhile, he continued to submit weekly reports to Shafter, listing the money as being "in transit."[23]

On August 5 Small telegraphed Flipper that he had not received the funds and again requested the transfer. When he received no reply, he telegraphed Shafter, informing him that funds reported by Flipper as mailed on July 9 had not been received. After consulting with Flipper, Shafter replied:

> Lieut. Flipper tells me three thousand seven hundred and ninety one dollars and seventy seven cents all in checks was mailed to your address July ninth. Books show that account transferred. No record of letter of transmittal or of number or description of checks. Lieut. Flipper states the letter endorsing this amount gave a description of each check and the amount for which it was drawn. Please telegraph me at once if it has not come to hand.[24]

When Small confirmed he had no such record, Shafter examined the books of the Subsistence Department, which showed $3,791.77 transferred to Small on July 9; it was listed "in transit" until the report for the week ending August 6, when it was dropped from the books. Flipper said he had no record of the checks or copy of the letter of transmittal, since he had handled the business in his quarters late at night and enclosed everything in an envelope addressed to Small, which he had mailed himself.

Because Flipper had failed to keep a record of the transaction, Shafter decided to relieve him the next morning, replacing him with Lt. Frank H. Edmunds, First Infantry.[25] He advised Small of the change, saying:

> Lieut. Flipper says he sent the checks and invoices in one package by mail July ninth. He kept no record of checks or letter of transmittal. The checks missing are dated between April seventeenth and July ninth & he says he endorsed to you. I have stopped payment on all checks to Flipper as A.C.S. between those dates. A large part of the amount was received from officers by check. Of all such I can get full description and forward by today's mail. . . . Lieut. Flipper has been a very good and attentive officer but his carelessness in this transaction is inexcusable.[26]

At this point, Shafter did not seem to think Flipper was guilty of anything besides gross negligence and sent him out with a verbal reprimand. That evening, however, as he and his wife were driving through the town of Fort Davis about a mile down the road from the post, he saw Flipper's horse with saddlebags attached, tied up in front of Sender and Siebenborn's store. The road through town also led to Mexico, and the more Shafter thought about it, the more he worried that Flipper might be trying to desert with the missing money. The adjutant, Lieutenant Wilhelmi, was sent to bring Flipper back to the post, where he was ordered to give Lieutenant Edmunds all public funds then in his possession, "something over two thousand dollars," before leaving his quarters. Shafter was also disturbed by Flipper's "very unconcerned manner" and by the fact that Flipper had not informed him of Small's first telegram of August 5.

The next morning, Shafter summoned Flipper to his quarters and said, "Mr. Flipper, I believe you stole that money. I may be doing you a grave injustice, and I hope I do. If so, I shall tell you so." He added that Flipper's check "represents nearly a year's pay of yours, and to your personal account to have no right to this amount. I shall immediately telegraph the bank to know if the check will be honored, and shall have your quarters searched." Flipper, according to one contemporary account, turned pale and said, "You are very unjust to me, colonel."

Wilhelmi and Edmunds reluctantly went to Flipper's quarters and began their search. In his desk, they found three hundred dollars with letters of transmittal, but this still left a very large deficiency of funds. They also recovered weekly statements for July, signed by Shafter but not mailed. They seized various articles of Flipper's personal property, including his West Point class ring. After informing Flipper he was under arrest and confined to quarters, Wilhelmi went into the hallway, where Edmunds told him he had noticed some cinders in the fireplace "which might be the remains of checks." Flipper was confined to his quarters under an armed guard, who was told to hold him incommunicado and not allow anything in the room to be disturbed. Then Wilhelmi reported to Shafter, who accompanied him back to Flipper's quarters.[27]

The arrest astonished the officers and their families. Captain Kinzie Bates's wife, Lillie, wrote, "The affair was talked over sub rosa yesterday, everybody sympathizing with Lieutenant Flipper, who was such a bright man, the man of his race in a certain respect, yet some thought it strange that the checks should be stolen from the mail, and stranger yet that he should neglect to have a memorandum of numbers and amounts." Nevertheless, she discounted the idea that he planned to desert to Mexico, commenting (as was later brought out in trial) that he frequently rode with his saddlebags. Besides, she said, "If Mr. Flipper contemplated a trip to Mexico he could have crossed the line before morning."[28]

Suspicion now turned toward Lucy Smith, Flipper's housemaid, whose belongings were found in his trunk. The officers found her cleaning when they arrived, and Shafter asked her if she knew Flipper was in trouble. She said she did not, nor did she claim to know anything about Flipper's business. Shafter ordered her back to his office, where a search yielded $2,853.56 in checks, of which $432.60 were negotiable, concealed in her clothing. Of these, $1,413.13 were checks given to Flipper by officers of the post in payment for June and July commissary bills, along with Flipper's check for $1,440.43. These were the checks Flipper had told Shafter were endorsed to Small and mailed on July 9. Lucy Smith was charged with theft of government property and sent to the county jail in Presidio (now Marfa), where she was interviewed before U.S. Commissioner J. J. Hartnett.[29]

Shafter was now convinced that Flipper had intended to embezzle the money. To department headquarters, he wrote:

> The amount embezzled by Lieut. Flipper is thirty seven hundred and ninety one dollars and seventy-seven cents. The checks of officers and money recovered today will reduce that amount fifteen or sixteen hundred dollars, [that] Lieut. Flipper has stolen. I have confined him in a cell in the post guard house, that being the only secure place on the post, until the orders of the Department Commander can be had in his case.[30]

The "cell in the post guard house" was a stone room 6½ feet long by 4½ feet wide. Although the door was shut, at any given time at least fifteen ordinary soldier-prisoners, confined on various charges, were housed in the corridor just outside. No visitors were allowed without Shafter's approval.[31]

Although Shafter had the legal right to confine Flipper, it was extremely unusual in the case of an officer. The army was still reeling from adverse publicity over the recently concluded Whittaker court-martial at West Point, which had prompted General Schofield's replacement as superintendent. The similarities between Shafter's treatment of Flipper and Schofield's mishandling of the Whittaker affair were all too apparent to generals and politicians still smarting over the Whittaker affair. On August 16, Shafter received a telegram from San Antonio stating, "The Commanding General [Augur] directs that you arrange for his security by providing a place other than the guard house."[32] In response, Shafter ordered Flipper returned to his quarters, where the back door and window were boarded up, and a hasp and lock were placed on the front door. The front window was nailed down. A sentinel on the front porch could look into the room.[33] A week later, Augur himself received a telegram stating the positions of Secretary of War Lincoln and General of the Army William Tecumseh Sherman. "Both the Secretary of War and the General of the Army require that this officer must have the same treatment as though he were white."[34] In other words, take off the lock, remove the boards, and place him under open arrest confined to post.

Meanwhile, the civilian business community of Fort Davis, which had come to respect Flipper during his tenure, rallied to his aid. A fund drive raised almost two thousand dollars toward the shortfall. Even Shafter gave one hundred dollars, although Flipper claimed the colonel made it a loan and kept his watch as security.[35] By August 17 Shafter was able to advise departmental headquarters that Flipper had turned in $3,056.38, including checks taken from Lucy Smith and money found in his room at the time of arrest.

He has given for the balance of his responsibility two due bills of perfectly responsible merchants of this place, due in ten days, one for two hundred (200)

dollars and one for four hundred and thirty five dollars
and thirty nine cents ($435.39) and a check of a respon-
sible party for one hundred (100) dollars on San Antonio National Bank to be paid at same time as due bills.
I consider the whole amount secure. I have taken the
sentinel off his room and placed Lieut. Flipper in close
arrest and until otherwise directed by the Department
Commander will continue him in that status.[36]

Twelve days later, Shafter reported Flipper had "made
good" all the money for which he was responsible. Edmunds
sent it to Small in San Antonio, asking that the negotiable
checks taken from Lucy Smith be kept by the bank, because
they would be needed as evidence. Shafter had filed two
charges against Flipper.[37] The first, consisting of only one specification, accused him of embezzling $3,791.77 in government
commissary funds entrusted to him as acting commissary of
subsistence, during the period of June 8 to August 13, 1881.

The second charge, conduct unbecoming an officer and a
gentleman, consisted of five specifications. The first stated
that, having been ordered by Colonel Shafter to transmit subsistence funds to the chief commissary, Flipper had, on or
about August 10, 1881, assured Shafter that the order had been
carried out, "well knowing the same to be false." The second,
third, and fourth were repetitious, the only difference being the
dates of the offenses. Judge Advocate General Swaim summed
them up in a report to Secretary of War Lincoln as follows:

> Presenting for approval to his said Commanding Offi-
> cer weekly statements of funds for which he [Flipper]
> was responsible as Acting Commissary of Subsis-
> tence, for the weeks ending July 9th, 16th and 23d,
> 1881, each containing the statement that said sum of
> money was "In transit to the Chief Commissary of
> Subsistence Department of Texas;" well knowing
> said statement to be false, in that said sum of money

was not in transit as stated, but had been retained by him or applied to his own use and benefit.

The fifth specification stated that Flipper had represented to Colonel Shafter, as part of the government funds, his personal check for $1,440.43, "which check was fraudulent and intended to deceive the said commanding officer."[38]

Each charge and specification was considered a separate offense. Verdicts were returned both on the charges and on each of the individual specifications.

In examining the Flipper case, one must consider that in 1881 Army Regulations recognized two different forms of embezzlement. One was *constructive* embezzlement, by which no actual misappropriation occurred. The accused was a custodian of government funds and had failed to handle them according to law or lawful instructions.[39] The other was *actual* embezzlement, by which the accused knowingly used or misappropriated government funds by any means other than that prescribed by law.[40] By these definitions, Flipper was, on the face of it, guilty of constructive embezzlement. The charge against him, however, stated that he "did embezzle, knowingly and willfully misappropriate and misapply public money of the United States, furnished and intended for the military service thereof."[41] In other words, he was charged with actual embezzlement, which would be much more difficult to prove, and which would hinder the government's case throughout the trial.

Why, then, was he charged with actual embezzlement, when conviction for constructive embezzlement would have been a foregone conclusion? The answer may lie with the Sixtieth Article of War, which addresses a member of the military who "steals embezzles, knowingly and willfully misappropriates, applies to his own use or benefit, or wrongfully or knowingly disposes of" government funds. In short, the charges appear to have been based on the Articles of War, without giving due consideration to the legal aspects of Army Regulations.[42]

If the charge of embezzlement was ambiguous, the second charge, "conduct unbecoming an officer and a gentleman," was the more dangerous to Flipper's military career. It was taken from the Sixty-first Article of War, a catchall that stated, "Any officer who is convicted of conduct unbecoming an officer and a gentleman shall be dismissed from the service." The definition of such conduct was at the discretion of the court-martial board trying the case.[43] In short, it was a means by which the army could rid itself of undesirable officers. Although many an individual officer found himself dismissed under this article, to the officer corps as a whole it was essential to the maintenance of good order. The corps imagined itself as an honor-bound institution, representing duty, morality, and good character. The Sixty-first Article of War, with its pointed use of the terms "officer" and "gentleman," was a means of self-policing to ensure these virtues were upheld.[44] Thus, as Flipper undoubtedly realized, a charge of misconduct held equal weight with a charge of embezzlement.

At Fort Concho, Colonel Grierson was concerned. "Lieut. Flipper has gotten into trouble at Davis about his money account or commissary or quartermaster and I learn he is to be tried by Court-Martial," he wrote to his wife, Alice, adding, "If not guilty of any dishonesty, I hope that he will be vindicated."[45]

Now, however, the story was beginning to attract national attention. The *Nation*, then a leading weekly journal, suggested Flipper take his cue from Whittaker. After printing a summary of the government's position against Flipper, it commented:

Such is the story sent out from Fort Davis, but what is Flipper's side of the story? Is he unfamiliar with the Whittaker case? Does he not know that the prejudice

in the army against colored officers is so intense that
there would be nothing unnatural in "putting up a
job" of this kind? Did he never suspect anything when
they pretended to like and esteem him very much,
and craftily made him commissary, and entrusted
him with funds, well knowing that the negro race is
not accustomed to complicated pecuniary transactions, and can easily be confused about them by
means of accounts, vouchers, and the like? When he
was suddenly called upon to account, and stated that
he had mailed his funds, did it never occur to him that
his servant might have been bribed, and the checks
carefully prepared to look like those which have disappeared and placed in his hands? Then the poor
defenceless boy is locked up, prevented from commu-
nicating with his friends, and stories are spread abroad
that his "most intimate associates of late have not
been the best." And this, too, at a distant post, surrounded by army officers who loathe him, graduates
of an institution where prejudice against his race is
cultivated by officers of instruction, and where the
mutilation of negro cadets [i.e., Whittaker] is regarded
as a platan pastime. It is pretty evident that Flipper
had not "retained counsel."[46]

Although the editorial was meant to be facetious, in part
to encourage the public "to suspend its judgment with regard
to the transaction until it knew the lieutenant's side of the
story; that he being a colored officer, the ordinary white view
of his conduct must not be taken as conclusive," some of its
readers did not take it that way. The *Nation* received letters
demanding to know if it was serious in the allegation. One,
outraged at the comparison to Whittaker, noted that the officers of both the Tenth Cavalry and the First Infantry, including Shafter himself, by and large were not West Pointers, but

had worked their way up the grades starting as volunteers in the Union army. Another wrote that Shafter "was one of the first, and was recognized in the army as one of the most successful, commanders of colored troops during the civil war."[47]

In Texas the *San Antonio Daily Express* took the racial issue much more seriously. In its September 7 issue, the *Express* noted unfair assumptions were being made about "the moral and intellectual status of the colored race" based on the examples of the three former West Pointers, Smith, Whittaker, and Flipper. Flipper, in particular, was being held up as representative of black soldiers as a whole, but the editorial added, "Such a rule would not be applied with any justice. Would the white people of this country like to be judged by an estimate of the character of some of their so-called representatives?"

That said, the *Express* went on to cite Flipper's overall commendable service record up to that point, commenting,

> but he fell, not through any lack of intelligence or sense of responsibility for offense committed, or because of any element in his nature peculiar to his people; but because of a failing, or inability for self-control, that has been found in many of the brightest men of all classes and all races, "There was a woman in it [i.e., Lucy Smith]." Flipper's fate has befallen thousands, and it never occurred to any one before to declare, because of the fall, that the race to which they belonged were incapable of that advanced and enlightened civilization accorded to others.[48]

Meanwhile, as the clouds gathered around Flipper, a court-martial board was organizing at Fort Stockton, to try another officer of the Tenth Cavalry, Capt. Thomas J. Spencer, for drunkenness on duty and conduct unbecoming an officer and a gentleman. In a letter to Alice, Grierson said both Spencer and Flipper wanted him to testify in their behalf, but he was trying to avoid it. "It is generally believed that Spencer will be dismissed. I hope so, but I trust that Flipper will not be as he has my earnest sympathy." He added he offered to write a letter "to be appended to the proceedings and commend him to the leniency of the court and the reviewing authority."[49]

The Spencer case is also significant in that several of the officers who participated in that trial became players in the Flipper court-martial almost immediately afterward.

4

THE COURT-MARTIAL BEGINS

Headquarters
Department of Texas
San Antonio, Texas, September 3, 1881
Special Orders
No. 108

I. A general court-martial will convene at Fort Davis, Texas, on Thursday, the 15th day of September, 1881, at 10 o'clock, A.M., or as soon thereafter as practicable, for the trial of Second Lieutenant H. O. Flipper, 10th Cavalry.

Detailed for the court:

Colonel G. Pennypacker, 16th Infantry;
Lieutenant-Colonel J. F. Wade, 10th Cavalry;
Major G. W. Schofield, 10th Cavalry;
Surgeon W. E. Waters, Medical Department;
Captain Fergus Walker, 1st Infantry;
Captain William Fletcher, 20th Infantry;
Captain W. N. Tisdale, 1st Infantry;
Captain R. G. Heiner, 1st Infantry;

Captain E. S. Ewing, 16th Infantry;
Captain L. O. Parker, 1st Infantry;
First Lieutenant W. V. Richards, Regimental Quarter-
master, 16th Infantry;
Captain J. W. Clous, 24th Infantry, is appointed judge-
advocate of the court.

No other officers than those named can be assembled
without manifest injury to the service.

By command of
Brigadier General Augur:
G. B. Russell,
Captain, 9th Infantry, A.D.C.[1]

To Colonel Grierson this order was extreme and unnecessary. At least once before, he had intervened to protect a
subordinate, in that case Captain Nolan, from court-martial
on charges preferred by Shafter, and there was no love lost
between the two colonels.[2] "I have made a strong appeal to
Gen. Augur for Court of Inquiry in Lieut. Flipper's case
instead of Court Martial," he told Alice, "but hardly think
the application will be granted."[3]

He was right. Augur responded by asking, "What would
be the use of a Court of Inquiry? So far as I have heard, there
is no dispute as to the correctness of the official reports made
in this case."[4]

Undeterred, Grierson strayed away from "the safe side"
in behalf of Flipper, who, after all, was a member of his regiment even if under Shafter's immediate command. Still push-
ing for an inquiry rather than a court-martial, he telegraphed
Augur:

Have not seen official reports in Lieut. Flipper's case,
I advised the course designated in view of full written
statement made by Lieut. Flipper to me and information received from various sources, and considering

the severe punishment already undergone, not for-
getting his successful struggle through West Point
and the excellent character he has bourne [sic] up to
the time of his present trouble and he as an officer
being the only representative of his race in the Army,
still believing it will be found that he has not committed any serious offense, I recommend that a Court
of Inquiry be appointed by yourself or the Secretary of
War to fully investigate all matters connected with
his case.[5]

Augur's reply indicated that he was finished discussing
the matter. "All the points you refer to can be, and in all
probability will be considered quite as carefully by a court-
martial, as by a court of inquiry," he told Grierson.[6] The subject was closed.

Those familiar with the recent television series *JAG* will
notice a profound difference between the conduct of the Flipper trial and the more modern approach portrayed by Holly-
wood. In the nineteenth century, the complex and detailed
Army Regulations were enforced under the much broader
Articles of War. The latter, adopted in 1806, were drawn from
the British Mutiny Act, which, in turn, had its origins in a
Swedish military code promulgated by King Gustav II Adolf
during the Thirty Years' War, nearly two centuries earlier.
Indeed, as Barry Johnson noted in *Flipper's Dismissal*, the
very seating arrangement of a U.S. court-martial in Flipper's
time adhered to Swedish regulations of 1620.

The vagueness and ambiguities of the Articles of War
were the subject of more or less continual question and discussion in the American military. Nevertheless, the Articles
under which Flipper was tried continued in use until 1950,
when they were replaced by the Uniform Code of Military
Justice, in an effort to bring military tribunals more into line
with those of the civilian world.[7]

The officer corps, from which court-martial boards were drawn, saw itself as an honorable institution. Whether or not this view was realistic, it did affect the conduct of trials when officers were defendants. These were courts of honor, in which an indictment against an officer and a gentlemen was tried by other officers and gentlemen, many of whom knew the defendant officer, if not personally, at least by name or reputation. The epaulettes on the defendant's shoulders (defendants appeared in full dress uniform as did the members of the court) and the fact that he possessed a congressional commission carried great weight and generally influenced the court to lean in his favor.

Yet there was a downside to this sense of honor. Throughout the army, there was a notion that officers were above dishonor in matters of government money. Charges concerning financial impropriety were unpleasant reminders of reality and therefore would have been considered particularly reprehensible. Thus, the emotions of the board trying Flipper would be pulled in two opposing directions.[8]

The composition of the court is worth noting. None of these officers were West Pointers, and all had served in the Civil War when Flipper was still a boy. The president of the court, Colonel Pennypacker, had thirteen years' seniority over Shafter in active Regular Army rank and had just come from Fort Stockton, where he presided over the Spencer trial. He was a hero, having received a near fatal wound during the assault on Fort Fisher, North Carolina, in 1865. His gallantry earned a brevet promotion to brigadier general at the age of twenty, too young even to vote. Two years later, he became the youngest man ever promoted to the active rank of full colonel in the Regular Army. He would have been one of the last people to be intimidated or bluffed by the irascible Shafter, and the court was subject to his immediate guidance.[9]

Pennypacker's health, however, was a concern. He never completely recovered from the bullet wound at Fort Fisher, and some officers and enlisted men felt his retirement was overdue. Indeed, he was too ill to attend all the sessions of the Spencer court-martial, and this appears to have created some concern about his ability to handle the Flipper case.[10]

Lieutenant Colonel Wade, commanding officer of Fort Stockton, and Major Schofield, designer of the Smith & Wesson Schofield Model revolver and brother of General Schofield, were the second and third senior ranking officers of Flipper's own regiment, and Captain Ewing was from Pennypacker's regiment. Much has been made of the fact that three of the officers were from Shafter's regiment (Captain Parker was relieved of court-martial duty before the trial began). Yet even here, the records are significant. Tisdale had been with the regiment for twenty years, and Walker and Heiner for more than a decade. Tisdale and Walker were senior captains. Walker had been breveted to major for gallantry during the Battle of Chancellorsville. Heiner, who most recently had served as Spencer's defense counsel, had entered the army as second lieutenant of a black infantry unit in 1863. These men hardly would have been any more impressed by Shafter than the others.[11]

Captain Clous, the judge advocate who would present the government's case, was an officer of Shafter's former regiment and had served with the colonel against Kiowas and Comanches in 1871. The previous December, he had been judge advocate in an officer's court-martial over which Colonel Pennypacker presided.[12]

Born in Württemberg in 1837, John Walter Clous immigrated to the United States, where he joined the army as a private and member of the band of the Ninth Infantry in February 1857. In 1862 he was commissioned second lieutenant of the Sixth Infantry, and earned brevets to first lieutenant and captain for gallant and meritorious service at Gettysburg a year later. Clous was promoted to the active rank of captain of the Thirty-eighth Infantry in 1867 and remained with the regiment when it was amalgamated with another black regiment to form the Twenty-fourth two years later. At some point during this period he studied law. His legal skills both as defense counsel and judge advocate developed to the point that, although he essentially was a field soldier, Augur's predecessor, General Ord, retained him in San Antonio as a staff officer, to try serious offenses within the Department of Texas.[13]

Although Flipper later contended that Clous stacked the deck by selecting members of the court, reviewing the proceedings after the trial, and recommending "the approval of his own work,"[14] this simply was not true. The board for a general court-martial was selected by the adjutant general of the department, in this case Col. Thomas Vincent, who as chief administrative officer knew which officers were available. Those selected for such boards generally belonged to the infantry, because they had less field duty on the Indian frontier than cavalry, and therefore more flexibility for assignment to detached duty. The record of testimony was reviewed at regular intervals during the trial, allowing each witness to make corrections, and permitting the defense and judge advocate to seek any necessary clarification. All arguments on points of law and procedure also were recorded and presumably read by the departmental commander, negating the need for Clous to review anything. As he himself noted at one point in the trial, the judge advocate "does not make the details and does not order the court."[15]

The only real disadvantage to Flipper was that in 1881 the judge advocate, as legal representative of the government, was privy to all closed sessions of the board—something the defense was not. A wise judge advocate could use those discussions to benefit the government's case.

Despite the generally bland official functions of the judge advocate, Clous's personality was a factor during the trial. Under the Articles of War, the judge advocate merely presented the government's case, administered all oaths, and questioned witnesses on behalf of the government. He was not a prosecutor in the civilian sense of the word. Clous, however, had a tendency to prosecute, an inclination that Flipper's defense counsel would encourage during the trial to establish a definite adversarial relationship.

The tendency to prosecute betrayed Clous's origins. Despite his years in the United States, he approached his cases with Teutonic thoroughness, a stickler for regulation and form. His guiding principle, as stated during the trial, was "If we follow the Regulations, we cannot go wrong." He was annoyed by the "brother officer" attitude of the court toward the defendant, by which Flipper's defense was allowed considerable leeway in presenting its case, and the defense played on this annoyance throughout the trial.[16]

Flipper's scenario for the selection of the board and approval of its findings was not based on ignorance; it was outright misrepresentation. Law was part of the first class curriculum at West Point, which Flipper himself described in *The Colored Cadet*. He knew the system, and in fact, among his other duties that summer, he served as judge advocate trying cases in general court-martial at Fort Davis. In July he had presented the government's case to a court-martial board that included Captains Bates and Charles Vielé and Lieutenants Wilhelmi and Edmunds, all of whom would testify against him in his own trial. It must have galled him considerably when Shafter received telegrams from San Antonio appointing the much despised Nordstrom as judge advocate "vice Flipper, relieved," and ordering him to "cause all untried charges referred to Lieut. Flipper to turn over to Lieut. Nordstrom, Judge Advocate, General Court Martial, for trial."[17]

United States v. *Henry Ossian Flipper* began in the post chapel/school building at Fort Davis at 11:00 A.M. September 17, 1881, two days behind schedule because Clous had been delayed by weather and bad roads. Since the delay had hindered his preparations, the court adjourned until September 19. When the proceedings resumed, Flipper was offered a chance to object to any member. If he had had any reservations about three of Shafter's men on the board, this would have been the chance to remove them, but he accepted the court as presented. This acceptance, normally an obscure part of the formalities, later would be disputed at length.[18]

With the preliminaries out of the way, Flipper was granted time to obtain counsel, and the court adjourned until 10:00 A.M. November 1.[19] He now had to find competent representation. Army trial procedures of the period are vague and contradictory as to whether he was entitled to an officer as a defense attorney as a right or merely as a courtesy. It is clear, however, that prior to 1890 no officer could be ordered to defend him.[20]

Civilian attorneys wanted at least a thousand dollars to take the case. When Flipper sent a white friend to the East to raise money, black leaders in the major cities politely declined to become involved. One can only imagine their reaction when Flipper, who had disdained any serious association with the African American community and its needs up until this point, suddenly approached it for help. His aloofness was coming back to haunt him.

Among those he contacted was John F. Quarles, the Ponder slave who had given him his basic education. Quarles was approximately ten years older than Flipper. After Emancipation, he came under the patronage of Charles Sumner, who arranged for him to attend Washington College in Pennsylvania. Upon graduation, he read law in Sumner's Washington, D.C., office, was admitted to the Georgia bar, and became a prominent attorney. He subsequently held consular posts in Málaga and Majorca. Returning to the United States in 1880, he settled in Flushing, on Long Island, where he was active in politics.[21]

On September 4, Flipper wrote to Quarles, who passed the letter on to the *Globe*. The New York newspaper published it, acknowledging:

It is a private letter and not intended for publication, but it is felt by the friends of Mr. Flipper that so much unfavorable comment has been made upon his case that his statement of it should not be withheld from the public. The letter is therefore published without his consent and against his wish.

In the letter, Flipper himself brought up the first mention of a conspiracy instigated by Colonel Shafter, who "professed great friendship" even while planning his ruin. In comments that he repeated almost verbatim over thirty years later in his 1916 memoir, he said he had been "several times warned against him" and "took every possible precaution to guard against him." Going over what he felt were Shafter's machinations, including a suggestion that Flipper make up the funds from amounts carried over from the previous fiscal year, he wrote, "You will observe here a deeply laid plan to entrap me, which I did not notice at the time, or I would have declined to turn over a single thing until I had put everything in condition."

Flipper then contended that Lucy Smith, cleaning up his quarters after the search, found the papers scattered about, and put them inside her dress for safekeeping. Upon recovering them from Lucy, Shafter supposedly said, "I've got him where I want him."

As for Nordstrom, Flipper wrote, "He hates me, and I have caught him at my window twice. He has trained his servant to watch me, and he watches me and my servant as closely as possible. . . . Even the colonel prowls around at night and has been seen at my windows."

Saying he wanted to be tried at Fort Davis, so he could avail himself of the witnesses on his behalf in that vicinity, Flipper concluded, "I am confident that I can win my case, and then the reaction in the public feeling will make up for the hard things being said now. Of what the colonel and the authorities have done I know only very little, and of what they intend to do I know nothing. A trap was set for me, into which I unwittingly stepped. I was taken by surprise, and not allowed one word of explanation."

The *Globe* accompanied the letter with its own editorial comment:

> Colonel Shafter may as well understand at once that the day Lieutenant Flipper is arraigned before his court-martial he will be arraigned before the country, and if Flipper is proved innocent by his court, [Shafter] will be adjudged guilty of the dastardly crime of attempting to destroy the reputation of a brother officer to gratify personal hate and prejudice.[22]

The letter also indicates some earlier correspondence over the possibility of Quarles representing Flipper, although Flipper told Quarles that he was "not able to bear any great expense."[23] The timing of the letter, with its allegations against Shafter and Nordstrom, is significant. It was written one day after the court-martial was ordered, and eleven days before the trial was scheduled to begin. One cannot escape the idea that Flipper already was preparing excuses for his actions.

The Quarles letter, or extracts, was reprinted in the *Nation*, the *San Antonio Daily Express*, and the *Army and Navy Journal*, which were available at the post library at Fort Davis, as well as in other New York and Washington papers. Shafter was furious, and his anger may have had some bearing on later, unsuccessful efforts to take Flipper to task in connection with his handling of accounts involving the deserter scout Charles Berger.[24]

Meanwhile, faced with indifference from the black community and feeling helpless, Flipper "determined to fight my battle alone and unaided, as I had always done, when, like a bolt out of a clear sky, I received a letter from Captain Merritt

Barber of the 16th Infantry, white, offering to come and defend me."[25] It is very unlikely that the offer came "like a bolt out of a clear sky," because Barber had a record of involvement in complicated and controversial cases, most recently as judge advocate for the Spencer court-martial.[26] In fact, Flipper even wrote to departmental headquarters in San Antonio requesting him, although it is unclear whether he and Barber already had communicated. Grierson was pleased with the idea, telling Flipper "to leave the entire management of your case to Captain Barber who is a good lawyer. To employ an outside citizen lawyer would be an unnecessary expense and do you more harm than good."[27]

Likewise, one cannot escape the notion that Barber's motives were less than altruistic. Although he was posted to Fort McKavett, some 250 miles to the east, he was rarely there during 1881 because he appears to have been one of the busiest legal officers in the army. Earlier in the year, he had been summoned all the way from Texas to New York, to serve as a member of the Whittaker court-martial board. After that came the Spencer case.[28]

Barber appears to have looked for situations that would take him away from the dreary, mundane life at Fort McKavett. Founded in 1852, McKavett developed into a large regimental post, with school, chapel, two parade grounds, and commodious quarters. By the early 1880s, however, it no longer served a purpose. The Indian troubles in west-central Texas essentially had ended, and although it remained headquarters of the Sixteenth Infantry, the garrison had been reduced to fewer than two hundred men, not counting their officers. The post was isolated, in an equally isolated part of the state, its only regular connection with the outside world being the mail service.[29] Small wonder, then, that Barber constantly watched for opportunities for reassignment. He mentioned to a friend that he wanted to retire.[30] Barring that, he apparently hoped at least for an assignment in the East.

A native of Vermont, and a year younger than Clous, Barber had attended Williams College. He was prepared for entry into the school by Chester A. Arthur, who at the time of the Flipper case was president of the United States, and with whom he appears to have maintained at least some association. Barber practiced law for three years prior to entering the army during the Civil War, and he had been breveted for gallantry during the Wilderness Campaign and at Cedar Creek. Besides serving as assistant adjutant general of Volunteers, he had also twice been regimental adjutant after entering the Regular Army in 1866. He was a skilled attorney in felony law and in military law.[31]

Following the Spencer case, Barber had applied for, and received, a thirty-day leave with an extension of an additional thirty days; therefore, he had no official status for the time being. For that reason, General Augur could not approve Flipper's request that Barber act as counsel, although he advised both Flipper and Barber that he would not object. Barber himself wanted to make sure that handling Flipper's case would not count against his leave time and was told the matter would be referred to the War Department. Additionally, under regulations, no formal orders could be given assigning Barber to Fort Davis for the trial, and no transportation could be ordered specifically for that purpose. On the other hand, if military transportation happened to be available at Fort McKavett, or was passing between McKavett and Fort Davis, Barber was free to use it.[32] Augur was doing everything possible, within regulations, to make certain that Flipper had adequate counsel.

"He came, lived in my quarters with me and made a brilliant defense, better than any civilian lawyer could have done," Flipper recalled more than thirty years later.[33]

Court reconvened as scheduled on November 1, with two additional officers, Lt. Col. James Van Voast, Sixteenth Infantry, and Col. David S. Stanley, Twenty-second Infantry, commanding officer of Fort Clark, detailed to the board on orders from General Augur. This was not an arbitrary decision. On October 13 Augur had advised the Adjutant General's Office he intended to augment the court with additional officers, saying, "When [the] Flipper court was ordered, officers of desirable rank were scarce." Since then, however, several had become available for detached duty, and he wanted to include them "as it is feared Colonel Pennypacker will be forced by ill health to leave." He saw nothing particularly out of line in the decision, pointing out the "[p]resent court has been sworn, but accused not arraigned."[34]

Flipper, however, objected, saying the orders that established the court-martial and appointed its members stated that "no other officer than those named could be assembled without manifest injury to the service." Arguing there was no valid reason for adding new members, he pointed out that he was offered the right to challenge the original members of the court; he had accepted them and by doing so had waived his right to further challenge. Now, having waived that right with the original members and being debarred from further challenges, he said that "a new element is infused into the court, which I had no reason to expect, and which I could not and did not take into consideration."[35]

Saying Flipper's challenge amounted to a challenge to the authority of the department commander, Clous got a recess to prepare his reply. When the court returned, he said the statement that no other officers could be assembled was a procedural phrase and irrelevant to the case. When Clous pointed out that Augur had consulted the War Department in the matter, however, Barber protested:

> The accused is not aware that the War Department is authorized to have anything to do with the composition of this court after the department commander has exercised his prerogative, and has selected the

court, and it has been organized, sworn in, been in deliberative sessions and has taken the interests of my client in its charge.

The record shows that the accused was satisfied with the court. The department commander was satisfied with the original detail when he made it, for he says no others could be assembled "without manifest injury to the service." The accused was satisfied when he was summoned before it because he accepted the detail without challenge. Consequently the court was organized. . . . Now some motive must have influenced a change in its composition, and the accused has the right to feel that the motive must have been adverse. . . . One member entirely changes the composition of the court, because [Flipper] did not consider that member.

After closed deliberation, the court upheld General Augur's right to appoint additional members but sustained Flipper's challenge to Van Voast and Stanley on the grounds of dissatisfaction. One might detect the hand of Colonel Pennypacker in at least part of the decision. Van Voast was the lieutenant colonel of his own regiment, and he may have felt that if both he and his second in command were away on court-martial duty, it might indeed constitute "manifest injury," if not to the service, at least to the Sixteenth Infantry. Van Voast and Stanley retired from the courtroom and from the trial.[36]

At this point, Clous noted that he had an "additional matter to be presented to this court for trial," which he said he only recently had been given. Consequently, he asked an adjournment to continue his preparations. Barber responded by asking the record to show that Flipper had been served with the relevant charges and was ready to go to trial. Nevertheless, court was adjourned for two days.[37]

Late the following day, Flipper was served with a new set of charges stemming from the Berger affair,[38] and when court reconvened on November 3, Barber was ready to fight. Clous, though, was one step ahead, saying it would not be proper to present these charges until after the current trial was concluded. If Flipper opted "to save time and the ordeal of two separate trials," and was willing to waive the right of challenge and have the court sworn again for the second set of charges, then Clous said he would have no objection to trying both sets of charges together. That said, Clous prepared to arraign Flipper on the original charges.[39]

Barber interjected that he needed to consult with Flipper on the new charges and obtained a recess. When it was over, he demanded to know the origin of the new charges, which during the previous session of court had not even been prepared. He did not rule out combining all charges in a single trial but stipulated that decision could not be made without further information.

Clous gave a noncommittal answer, but when Barber continued to press his demand, the judge advocate finally replied:

> I will state that the charges and specifications that I have referred to in my remarks were prepared and are signed by Colonel William R. Shafter, First Infantry. That these charges have been handed me with an order to bring them before this court, and they have been approved and ordered for trial by the department commander. I presume that information will be sufficient.[40]

The arguments continued into the afternoon and were getting nowhere. Finally, Barber said Flipper was not prepared to answer on separate trials at that point. He then asked for a list of papers and property taken from Flipper's quarters at the time of his arrest, in order to determine witnesses to call for the defense. He said that both he and Flipper had asked Shafter for the list and that Shafter had repeatedly assured them it would be provided. Barber said Shafter ultimately admitted he had given the list to Clous.[41]

Clous replied that an argument in court was a waste of time. He pointed out that Army Regulations prescribed how witnesses were procured, and if Barber wanted any papers or witnesses, he should make proper application. Only if Clous then failed to provide them should the matter be brought up before the court. Until that time, Clous said, "There is no use of taking up the time of the court about this matter and lumbering up the record."

"We don't know what papers you have got," Barber argued.

"You can address me on the subject, and I will give you a list of all the papers I have got," Clous said. "There is no use of lumbering up the record in that way. When I fail in that respect to do the duty imposed on me by the regulations of the army, then I think, is time enough for the accused to come before this court and complain, but not now. I have not been asked heretofore. The first official information I have had is from the accused, just now, in court."[42]

Barber apologized but said he had reason to believe Clous had documents that were material in the defense, and that would help Flipper determine witnesses to summon. But when he asked the court "to instruct the judge-advocate or request him" to furnish the list,[43] Clous bristled and told Colonel Pennypacker:

> Mr. President, I again say that it is not competent for this court to take any action upon that subject until I have failed to do my duty, and I consider the request as a reflection upon me in a matter upon which I have not been asked to act. On the contrary, when I came here first to try this case, I showed him every paper I

had in my possession, and since that [time] I have informed his counsel outside of court that whenever he wished to ask me about any paper I would be very glad to show it to him, and I ask the court to be cleared now to settle the matter.[44]

Barber acknowledged that Clous had cooperated up to that point and said he would henceforth confer with the judge advocate before bringing such matters up. Pennypacker, apparently irritated with the slow progress of the proceedings, said the time had come to arraign Flipper on the original charges. At Barber's request the arraignment was postponed until the following morning.[45] Although Barber had moderated his tone toward the end of the session, the arguments throughout the day foreshadowed the carefully orchestrated rancor that would develop between him and Clous as the trial progressed.

5

Shafter on the Defensive

When court reconvened, Flipper said he would agree to be tried on the original charges and those from the Berger affair in the same court-martial, and he waived the right of challenge. Clous apparently now was having second thoughts because, after a closed session, he responded that since Flipper's statement was not in the form of a motion or a proposition, the government intended to proceed only on the original charges and specifications and would try the new charges at a later date.

Flipper then was arraigned for embezzlement with one specification and for conduct unbecoming an officer and a gentleman with five specifications. He pleaded not guilty to each charge and specification.[1]

As government exhibits, Clous submitted Flipper's accounts current for June and July and his return of provisions for August, all of which were verified by the defendant.[2] The government then called its first witness, Colonel Shafter. Under the rules, Clous would conduct the examination-in-chief of government witnesses, with Barber restricting his cross-examination to points raised by the judge advocate. If Barber wished to move into new areas, then he was free to recall the witnesses on behalf of the defense. With defense witnesses, the roles were reversed, with Barber conducting the examination-in-chief and Clous cross-examining.

Under questioning by Clous, Shafter went over events up until the time Small notified him the money had not been received in San Antonio.[3] He said when he asked Flipper why Small's earlier message on missing funds had been withheld, Flipper replied "that he thought it was only some temporary delay in the mail, that [the money] would reach San Antonio soon, and that it was not worthwhile to trouble me about it. I think all that I said to him then was that I preferred to be troubled about such matters and that he should have notified me." He described Flipper's explanation about how the checks and invoices had been mailed and said at that point he had relieved Flipper as ACS.

Shafter went on to say that on August 12, he had confronted Flipper about the money, including his personal check for $1,440.43, which was not on the list of checks Flipper claimed had been sent. When Flipper said he had forgotten it, Shafter testified, "I told him that was a very large sized check to forget, that I did not believe he had ever sent the checks and that I was going to act accordingly, that if I was doing him an injustice I would apologize to him when it was over, and if I was not, I did not care anything about it."[4]

Shafter then discussed the search of Flipper's quarters, his arrest, the interview with Lucy Smith, and the recovery of more than $2,800 in checks found in her possession. Several of these he recognized as having been presented to him as commanding officer on July 8, the day before he ordered them sent to San Antonio. Among those was Flipper's check for $1,440.43. After exchanging telegrams with the bank, Shafter said he went to see Flipper in the guardhouse and told him he "has no personal account with the bank and consequently his check for $1,440.00 was good for nothing, and that his deficiency, instead of being about $900, was perhaps something like $2,300.00 or $2,400.00."

According to Shafter, Flipper replied, "Yes, Colonel, I had to deceive you in the matter in some way and I took that way to do it." Shafter said he then told Flipper, "[Y]ou need not incriminate yourself—I don't want you to do so unless you choose to, but I should like to know where that money has gone to, if you are willing to tell me."

"He said, 'Colonel, I don't know where it has gone to,'" Shafter continued. "I said, 'It is very strange that you should be short $2,400.00 and not know where it is, or what has become of it.'"

"Yes, that is so, but I can't account for it unless some of them have stolen it from me," Flipper supposedly replied, to which Shafter asked, "Who do you mean by 'some of them'?"

When Flipper said he did not know, Shafter asked him if he thought Lucy Smith might have any of it. "He said, 'No, sir, I do not.'"[5]

At Flipper's request, Shafter said he met with three area merchants and citizens of Fort Davis, who Flipper felt would help make up the deficit. After visiting him in the guardhouse, the three asked Shafter about Flipper's situation if the money were repaid. Shafter said he told them it would save him from prison and that as soon as the amount was repaid, "I should release him from the guard house and place him in his quarters as I would any other officer that was under arrest." Here Shafter indicated that it was repayment of the money, rather than orders from superiors, that led to Flipper's release.[6]

Under cross-examination by Barber, Shafter said he had relieved Flipper as quartermaster almost immediately after assuming command of Fort Davis, since he planned to appoint his own regimental quartermaster to the position.

From then until August 10, Flipper had continued to serve as commissary, and Shafter acknowledged he believed Flipper had performed those duties "intelligently and entirely to my satisfaction" until the cash shortage arose. He added that about July 1 he told Flipper he planned to relieve him from commissary duties "not because I was dissatisfied with him, but because I thought he ought to be assisting other cavalry officers in performing their duties in the field."[7]

"Then," Barber began, "if I understand you correctly, that up to the occurance [sic] of this matter, the conduct of Lieutenant Flipper in the transaction of his official business with you was not only satisfactory but praiseworthy?"

"I say so, as far as I knew," Shafter replied.[8]

Barber then questioned Shafter about Small's absence from San Antonio, the delay in transmitting funds, and his conversation with Flipper about keeping such large amounts on hand. As Barber pressed for more details, Shafter admitted he did not know about procedures at Fort Davis prior to his assuming command and did not even know whether records or accounts for the previous command existed, because he had not bothered to look for them. He also admitted he had received no notice of deficiencies in Flipper's transmissions prior to July and added, "Up to that day there was no reason to think but that they were all straight."[9]

Shafter said that he did not know when Small's order to hold funds at Fort Davis was received, but that it came "two or three months" before the funds were ordered sent.

"After that time, did you inspect the funds regularly?" Barber asked.

"Every week when I was present, every Sunday morning—the funds on hand, not in his bank account," Shafter replied.[10]

By the time the court adjourned for the day, the *San Antonio Daily Express* noted, "The cross-examination did not elicit anything, save to strengthening [sic] the prosecution by more positive statements."[11] Yet as the day drew to a close, Barber was beginning to find cracks in Shafter's administration of Fort Davis that, in turn, might have affected Flipper's performance as commissary.

When cross-examination resumed the following day, Barber referred to a point in Clous's examination, asking why Shafter had obtained a list of checks from officers who had made commissary payments.

"It was taken," Shafter said, "because at the time—that I believed that the checks had been mailed, and by some means they had been lost in transit to the chief commissary at San Antonio, and I wished to get a list of the checks so that I could . . . have payments stopped on them." He added that Flipper's failure to include his own $1,400 check was among the things that caused him to think the checks had not been sent, "and learning that there had not been any stage robbery was another, Lieutenant Flipper's manner was another."[12]

Shafter was beginning to stumble, and Barber decided to go back over his testimony on the search of Flipper's quarters and his arrest. Now Shafter could no longer remember whether he looked at the papers Lieutenant Wilhelmi brought from Flipper's quarters or took Wilhelmi's word as to their contents.[13]

As Barber led him into the search of Flipper's person, Shafter said he had instructed Wilhelmi and Lieutenant Edmunds to see if he was concealing money. "If he had [they were ordered] to take it. Commissary funds were found on his person as I am told."

"Do you consider his watch commissary funds?" Barber inquired.

"No, sir, [I] consider it personal property."

"That is what I desire to call your attention to," Barber said, "whether your orders to these officers to search his room and his person, and take possession of his valuables, included such articles of ornament and use as were on his person."

"I told them to take possession of everything valuable about Lieutenant Flipper's quarters, and search him and see if he had any money, and in doing that, they took his watch—they obeyed my order exactly. They were expected to bring everything that was valuable about his place and person, and it was brought to my office and locked up and, except for the commissary funds that were found on his person, it is there yet and likely to stay there," Shafter snapped.

"That, Colonel, was not asked for by the question," Barber said.

"I know it was not," Shafter replied, now clearly on the defensive.

Barber said he understood the colonel's orders "included his watch, his finger rings, his shirt studs, his sleeve buttons, his shoe buckles and other articles of personal use and ornament that were found on his person at the time."

"There was nothing designated," Shafter explained. "I directed them to take possession of everything of value. I did not tell them to take his watch, mentioning it was a watch, or his shoe buckles, but told them to take possession of everything—to search and take possession of everything valuable that they found in his quarters and on his person."

"Please answer the question definitely," Barber said.

"I have answered it, sir," Shafter insisted.

"Did the scope of your orders intend to justify the taking of those articles of personal use and ornament which he had on his person at the time? Do you mean to be so understood?"

"I do mean to be so understood," Shafter said, "That I meant that they should take everything that he would not require in the guard house, as that was where I intended to place him and, as I did not want him to have his valuables there, and took them for safekeeping."

If that was the case, Barber asked why Flipper's belongings were not returned when he was released from the guardhouse. Shafter answered that Flipper had applied for them but

"I sent him back an endorsement of the message that I had just discovered one or two new steals [sic] as soon as that money was made good he could have his things. Mr. Flipper said that if he could be permitted to go to town he would raise the money that he had obtained of the commissary sergeant and—"

"Are you using his language?" Barber interrupted.

"I am using my own," Shafter replied. "I am using Mr. Flipper's language as given to me, as reported to me by an officer that I sent over to see him."

"Ah!" Barber countered. "You don't pretend then to give it of your own knowledge—the language of Lieutenant Flipper?"

"I do not, but I will tell you what occurred. I did give Lieutenant Flipper permission to go to town. He did so and paid the money, and then the officer went over to his quarters and told him he could have these things and he declined to take them except through civil proceedings. The things are left there yet, and I determined not to turn him over the things unless he called for them."[14]

Shafter was becoming unnerved. Barber, determined to make the most of it, turned to the interrogation of Lucy Smith.

According to Shafter, he had questioned her, then told her he was evicting her from the post and that the provost sergeant would pick up her belongings and escort her outside the military reservation.[15] She was leaving when his orderly said she was concealing papers in her dress. Shafter said he called her back and asked her if she was carrying any papers.

"She said, 'No, sir, I have not,'" Shafter testified. "She said, 'You can see I have not,' and she pulled her dress open and disclosed the inside of her dress. I said, 'Very well.' I simply looked as I sat across my desk. She was three or four feet off."

When the orderly still insisted Lucy was carrying the papers, Shafter said, he felt her dress on the side he had not seen and discovered the packages containing some of the missing checks. Shafter informed her that he was going to press charges against her and that she probably would go to prison.[16] Thus far, Shafter's testimony closely matched the affidavits both he and Lucy had given to the U.S. commissioner.

"Your affidavit, then, was based on the facts which she had told you in regard to the matter?" Barber asked.

"No, sir," Shafter replied. "My affidavit was based upon the fact that I found in her possession the property of the United States and that she was not the lawful custodian of that property, and had no right to have it."[17]

Barber then made his point, which was to challenge both Shafter's affidavit to the U.S. commissioner and his statements to the court that the interview with Lucy had been handled with propriety.

"I have given the substance of the language, and very nearly—as near as I can recollect—the exact language," Shafter insisted.

"Did you not use very violent language in your intercourse with Lucy on that occasion?" Barker asked.

"I did not."

"Did you not curse her?"

"I did not."

"Did you not threaten her?"

"I did not."

"Did you not refer in your language in abusive terms to improper relations between her and Lieutenant Flipper?" Barber asked.

"I did not," Shafter insisted. "I don't think I used an oath during the whole examination, although I am liable to, but I am very positive that I did not. On the contrary, I am sure that I talked very quietly to the girl. There were two or three persons present who heard the whole conversation."[18]

Barber was hitting points where Shafter was vulnerable; the colonel's bombast, threats, and profanity were well known in the army and had earned him little affection among his officers and men.[19]

Continuing this line of questioning, Barber asked, "After finding all the checks, have you stated all the action which you took toward Lucy?" Here Shafter was penned into a corner. Answering first in the affirmative, he then reconsidered and admitted he had sent for his own female servant and ordered her to take Lucy into another room and search her.

"Did you direct her to strip Lucy?"

"I directed her to make a thorough search."

"Do you swear that you did not order her to be stripped naked?"

"I did not tell her to be stripped, but I did tell the woman to examine every part of her clothing and see that there was nothing under them," Shafter replied.

"Do you know if that was done?"

"I know that the woman told me that it was done. She told me that she made her take all her clothes off."

"Where was this done?" Barber asked.

"In my own office."

"How many persons were around the office?"

"There was no person about the office whatever but the two women," Shafter said. "About the building there was probably the regimental quartermaster, sergeant major, my orderly, and perhaps others."

When Barber asked if any soldiers were watching through the windows, Shafter replied, "I don't know. I am very positive none were at the front windows and I don't believe there was any at the back."[20]

Although Shafter's affidavit to the commissioner acknowledged that he had threatened Lucy with a strip search, this was the first mention that one actually had occurred and that there may have been male spectators. For Victorian era America, where physicians routinely delivered babies under a blanket to avoid viewing the mother's body, a strip search was even more traumatic than it is today. Had Lucy Smith been white, it is debatable whether Shafter could have saved his career. As it was, his morals now were in question, and after a recess for lunch, Barber struck hard.

"Did not you tell her during that interview that if she would tell all she knew about Flipper, and tell the truth about this matter, she could have a house in the garrison, or quarters in the garrison here, and have friends among the officers, and that you would go around and see her yourself once in awhile?" he asked.

"I did not tell her any part of it, nor anything that could be tortured into it," Shafter said.

"You have stated that you did not use any violence or abusive language during that interview. . . . Did you not say to her during that interview, 'Yes, God damn you, you will go to the penitentiary, and Mr. Flipper, God damn him, I have got him where I want him'?"

"No, sir, I did not say anything at all like it except to tell her that she would probably wind up in the penitentiary, or would probably go to the penitentiary for her share of the transaction, but as far as cursing her, or swearing about Lieutenant Flipper to her, I did not do it," Shafter insisted.[21]

Barber now was trying to establish that Shafter had subjected Lucy to blatant sexual harassment, a line of questioning for which he probably had no grounds whatsoever. There was nothing in either Shafter's or Lucy's depositions to indicate that anything of that nature had occurred; nor would any subsequent testimony bring out that Shafter had said anything that could be construed as an indecent threat or proposition. Apparently Barber was using the now acknowledged strip search as a basis, allowing the imaginations of the court to follow through and totally discredit Shafter's testimony. All the while, Clous sat quietly, raising no objection. Possibly he had his own agenda, hoping that Barber's insulting cross-examination of a ranking field officer would alienate the court.

But when Barber went into Shafter's seizure of Lucy's personal effects, he protested the materiality and demanded Barber stick to things brought out in the examination-in-chief. Barber replied that it was open to cross-examination because Clous had questioned Shafter about his interview with Lucy.

Clous withdrew the objection, saying he wished to give the defense every opportunity to make its case. As Barber continued to press Shafter about specific personal items, however, Clous said he was going too far, and insisted on a ruling from the court. Barber, on the other hand, insisted on the question. After a conference in closed session, Clous's objection was sustained.[22]

Now Barber began questioning Shafter on Flipper's confinement in the guardhouse, trying to draw out that his basic needs were not met. Once again, Clous objected.

"Whom are we trying?" the judge advocate demanded. "This witness or the accused?"[23]

Frustrated, Barber replied, "We are not endeavoring to put the witness on trial before this court, but we are endeavoring to show that the treatment which had been administered to us has been the severest punishment that has been administered to an officer of the army since its organization."[24]

Clous's objection was overruled. Barber, however, already had made his point, and the rest of his questioning was routine. Court finally adjourned for the day at 3 P.M.[25] It had been a hard, brutal session. Commenting on it, the *San Antonio Daily Express* noted: "The defense is endeavoring to show that in the treatment of Lieut. Flipper . . . Col. Shafter was prompted by a persecuting spirit, not warranted by custom in the army in like cases, or the facts as they expect to develop them in due time."[26]

The sixth day opened with a forty-five-minute argument between Clous and Barber over the means and methods for summoning defense witnesses. When it was over, the court ruled for Barber, and Clous had such a headache he said he would be unable "to sit here any longer." Colonel Penny-packer offered to adjourn, but Clous said a recess, allowing him to rest for a while, would suffice. Court recessed for just over an hour, after which Shafter was recalled.[27]

Barber asked Shafter if he had any opinion of how Flipper might have used the missing money. The colonel admitted that "Mr. Flipper's habits had been such that he had not used it up himself. He was not a gambler, or was not known to be, and was not a drunkard, or was not known to be, and I knew no way how he could have got away with that amount of money, and consequently it was a mystery to me then and is to a very great extent now."

Moving to the citizen fund drive, Barber asked, "Was not their action in making up this amount of money influenced by your belief in the innocence of any guilt on the part of Lieutenant Flipper conveyed to them on that occasion?"

"I don't know what influenced them to do it," Shafter replied. He added that while he personally was convinced of Flipper's guilt, and had been at the time mentioned, he might have said something to the effect that he did not know how Flipper had managed to steal the money.[28]

Once again, as on the previous day, Barber started to go over Flipper's confinement in the guardhouse. Shafter acknowledged that no one could visit Flipper without his permission, but said the citizens of Fort Davis could visit as often as they wished, to discuss ways of making up the missing funds.

Saying he intended to control visits to Flipper and subjects discussed during those visits, the colonel testified, "I did think it best to permit him to be interviewed on the subject matter of his shortage, and continued it as long as it was necessary. I don't recollect of giving any permission to see him on any other subject."

When Barber asked if he specifically recalled denying anyone permission to visit Flipper, Shafter said he believed there had been "a number of persons." The only incident he specifically recalled was when "[a] colored man in town that has some official position asked to see him. . . . I asked him what he wanted. He said he wanted to see him. I told him he could not do it. I don't recollect any other, although there might have been."[29]

"Do you remember of any persons bringing a note of introduction from the United States Commissioner, who requested to see Lieutenant Flipper?" Barber asked.

"I do not."

"If such occurred, would you remember it?"

"Perhaps I might and perhaps not. I don't recollect it at this time."

Barber showed him the note, which then was handed to Clous for examination. Shafter asked that the note be read to him, then stated he still did not recall the incident, but added that based on the note alone, permission would have been denied.

"Do not you remember that a man presented that note from the commissioner, asking for an interview with Lieutenant Flipper, which you not only denied but sent the man out of the garrison?" Barber asked.

"I know positive that there was no man sent," Shafter replied, then hesitated. "Well, I should like to amend my answer, I recollect the whole thing now. There was a drunken nigger that had been a servant in the garrison. He came to me drunk and asked to see Flipper. . . . I told him he could not see Flipper. It was a drunken, worthless fellow that was very much intoxicated at the time, who could have no possible reason for seeing him. I cannot give his name without some person can tell it to me. But that is a fact."[30]

Barber ignored the racial slur, which mattered little in a nineteenth-century court, and pressed Shafter on the memory lapse. Ultimately, Shafter admitted that his memory was faulty on some points, adding he only remembered important events in the day-to-day administration of the post.

"You don't consider that the denial of a person in the guard house the privilege of seeing his friends, or the denial of his friends of seeing him, worthy of your recollection of the post?" Barber asked.

"I think I said that I did not recollect every little incident connected with the command of my post," Shafter replied. "I do now recollect this occurrence and that I did not consider it a hardship, or that it was a hardship for Lieutenant Flipper not to see this particular man, and I did not intend, as I have said before, that he should see any person unless I know about it, and it was on proper business."

On that note, court adjourned for the weekend.[31]

Henry Flipper in a West Point class photo taken four years before the
trial. Courtesy of Fort Davis National Historic Site.

Fort Davis from the north. The chapel, where the trial was conducted, is top center, facing the parade ground. Officers' row is on the right. Courtesy Fort Davis National Historic Site.

The Fort Davis post chapel served as a courtroom. This photo probably was made after Fort Davis was abandoned (note the broken windows) but the building would have appeared essentially the same at the time of the trial. Courtesy of Fort Davis National Historic Site.

Capt. Merritt Barber, defense attorney. Courtesy of Fort Davis National Historic Site.

John W. Clous, judge advocate, shown here years later as judge advocate general. Courtesy of Fort Davis National Historic Site.

Col. Benjamin Grierson. Courtesy Fort Davis National Historic Site.

William R. Shafter, here as a major general around the time of the Spanish-American War, when Flipper suggested that Shafter might help him get reinstated. Courtesy of Fort Davis National Historic Site.

Galusha Pennypacker, president of the court, shown here with his Union army brevet rank of major general. Courtesy of the National Archives.

Gen. Christopher C. Augur, the departmental commander who tried to reinstate the embezzlement charge. Courtesy of the National Archives.

Judge Advocate General David G. Swaim, who recommended leniency in the sentence. Courtesy of the National Archives.

President Chester A. Arthur. Courtesy of the author.

Ruins of the post chapel at Fort Davis. The plaque discusses the Flipper trial. Courtesy of the author.

Henry O. Flipper in the 1890s. Courtesy of Arizona Historical Society, Tucson, No. B3739.

Flipper's passport photo, ca. 1920. Courtesy of Fort Davis National Historic Site.

6

A Question of Persecution
and a "Mexican Theory"

When the trial reconvened on Monday, the seventh day, Barber and Clous got into another argument over the procedure for witnesses. This left Clous with another headache, and once again, court adjourned for slightly over an hour to allow him to rest. Upon reconvening, Shafter was recalled and Barber once again went over Flipper's confinement, this time in his quarters.[1]

The line of questioning had long since become redundant, and a member of the court (who was not identified in the record) had grown tired of it, saying that he had other government duties to perform and that he had been

> sent here for a particular purpose, that being to try Lieutenant Flipper for certain offenses. If there is an attempt to make out here a case of persecution, and that these acts of persecution were co-existent with the offense that may have been committed, I could see it at once, because I am a believer in the theory

95

that persecution may, in a manner, have caused the accused to have committed certain acts.

In making this statement, the member of the court was effectively inviting Flipper to prove the conspiracy and entrapment that, over the next five decades, he would claim had been prepared by Shafter and others. The member was saying he would consider it a mitigating factor in any offenses Flipper might have committed, and doubtless would have encouraged the other members of the court to do likewise. As it was, everything mentioned during the past two days of testimony occurred after the supposed commission of the acts charged, and he could see no bearing on Flipper's innocence or guilt. In other words, anything that might be construed as racism occurred *after* Flipper's arrest. There had been no indication of racism *prior* to the arrest.[2]

Barber replied that the charge of the Sixty-first Article of War, concerning conduct unbecoming an officer, required an examination of all circumstances of the case. He pointed out that Flipper, an officer not yet convicted of any offense, was "confined in a felon's cell" during five days of the hottest month of the year, along with more than sixteen common soldier-prisoners at any given time.

"I scarcely know how to present a reply to a member of the court, excepting to hope that no member of the court will feel that he has any other duties more important than those to defend and guard the integrity of a brother officer in the army," he said.[3]

The member acknowledged Barber's point and said that although he still doubted relevancy, he would withdraw his objection.[4] Even so, either Barber missed the chance to prove prior persecution and entrapment, which is unlikely considering his legal skill, or he could not prove that Flipper was the victim of a racist conspiracy in the first place.

In fact, Barber's defense was nothing but a technicality, adhering to the old law school adage "If you can't pound the facts, pound the law; if you can't pound the law, pound the facts; and, if you can't pound either, pound the table." Even if innocent of embezzlement, Flipper obviously was guilty of misconduct, and the only recourse was to attack the prosecution and find a hole in the case. Thus, Barber dwelt on his confinement in an effort to reveal a vicious side of Shafter's personality—a side that might have frightened Flipper into falsifying records rather than facing the colonel with the truth. Had Barber openly raised this point, however, he would have been admitting guilt. And he still could not have shown that Shafter was out to "get" Flipper from the moment he assumed command of Fort Davis. On the question of misconduct, Barber was pounding the table.

On the other hand, he could establish that the colonel was far from conscientious in performance of his own duties as post commander. He introduced the weekly statements for June, one prepared for Captain Bates's signature as acting commander in Shafter's absence and the other three, for Shafter's signature; none had been signed. Asked to explain this, Shafter said:

> I am positive that I always signed the statements when I examined the funds, and at no other time. It is possible that it may have been entirely forgotten and the Sunday passed by without me counting them, but if I was at the post, and my name is to the weekly statement, I know that I counted the funds rendered on that weekly statement.[5]

The catch was that an entire month had passed with no one's signature on the weekly statement, meaning, by Shafter's own admission, the funds for that month may not have been examined at all by the responsible command personnel. Barber was to hammer away at this point again and again throughout the trial.

Barber finished his cross-examination of Shafter on the ninth day, and after a brief reexamination by Clous and a few questions from the court, the colonel was excused. During the grueling days of examination and cross-examination, Shafter was revealed as a sloppy administrator, a racist, and an autocrat. Yet it was also obvious that Shafter initially entered his investigation convinced of Flipper's innocence and only later came to believe that he had stolen the money. If Barber wanted to show a conspiracy to entrap Flipper, he would have to look elsewhere.

On the tenth day of the trial, the government called Major Small, the departmental chief commissary of subsistence. Most of his testimony simply was a review of the irregularities in Flipper's account for the period of July 4 through 24, when Small was absent from San Antonio, and the subsequent efforts to resolve the differences between departmental headquarters and Fort Davis. In cross-examination, Barber brought out that Small had become chief commissary on December 20 of the previous year and that Flipper, already acting commissary of subsistence at Fort Davis, had come under his supervision at the time. Small testified:

> To the best of my knowledge, up to the time Lieutenant Flipper got into this trouble, [the business of the commissary] was well conducted. . . . I had no reason to be dissatisfied with the administration of the Subsistence affairs at this post up to the time Lieutenant Flipper got into trouble in any manner, shape or form. It was well conducted as far as I am aware, the duties were well administered.[6]

Small was excused about 12:40 P.M. After a break for lunch, his chief clerk in San Antonio, George Davidson, answered a few questions concerning transmission of funds during Small's absence from San Antonio. Barber did not cross-examine.[7]

The next witness was John Withers, cashier of the San Antonio National Bank, against which Flipper had drawn the

check for $1,440.43. Withers testified that Flipper had nei-
ther a personal account nor an account as ACS at the bank.
Under cross-examination from Barber, however, he acknowledged that Flipper had maintained a quartermaster's account
for about three months but had closed it in March. He also
stated that on August 17, when he had notified Shafter that
Flipper had no personal account per se, the bank was holding
a seventy-four-dollar certificate of deposit in his name, which
had been sent by his publisher—the royalty that Flipper
claimed he was expecting to cover his check.[8]

With that, the court adjourned for the day. The following
morning, the government planned to call one of its chief witnesses, Lt. Louis Wilhelmi, post adjutant.

Discussing the events leading to Flipper's arrest, Wilhelmi testified that on July 3 he overheard Shafter and Flipper discussing the $1,400 check and recalled Shafter as
saying, "Is not this check for $1,440 a very large amount for
an officer to have?" To that, Flipper supposedly replied, "Yes,
I had a lot of small checks which I did not wish to transmit,
or could not, to the chief commissary of the department, and
I sent them to the San Antonio National Bank for deposit.
This check represents that amount."

According to Wilhelmi, the date of that discussion was
"clearly fixed in my mind as the following day was the fourth
[of July] and Lieutenant Flipper had issued a circular asking
the Mexicans about Fort Davis—"

When Barber objected, Clous responded that Wilhelmi
was simply trying to say why he remembered the specific
dates.

Picking up in midsentence, Wilhelmi continued, "to
bring their burros here for a race on—"

This was too much for Barber, who said if Wilhelmi per-
sisted, he would ask protection of the court. It was obvious to
him that Wilhelmi and Shafter were trying to show that Flipper had plotted to abscond to Mexico with the missing

money, and he objected "to anything about Lieutenant Flipper issuing a circular for the Mexicans," contending it was not relevant.

"It is perfectly competent for him to give the conversation that he had with the accused in that connection," Clous responded, "and I presume he is simply giving the introductory remarks."

Colonel Pennypacker intervened, saying Wilhelmi could continue his statement and Barber could object to any part of the testimony as he saw fit.[9]

I will not take up the time of the court," Barber replied. "Let him slash it all in, if he wants to."

Wilhelmi concluded by saying that after Flipper and Shafter had finished, he and Flipper had discussed the race that was to occur on the Fourth. After describing the communications with San Antonio and the discrepancies in Flipper's accounts, Wilhelmi said that shortly before retreat on August 10, Shafter had observed Flipper's horse with saddlebags tied up in front of Sender and Seibenborn's store in town and was afraid Flipper "might leave the post, and the country." Shafter ordered him to ride over, inform Flipper he was relieved as acting commissary of subsistence, and bring him back to the post. Wilhelmi was also told to notify Lieutenant Edmunds that he was to obtain the commissary funds from Flipper and give him a receipt.[10]

Wilhelmi carried out his instructions, and upon their return to the post, Edmunds went to Flipper's quarters to arrange the transfer of funds. Moving on to the search of Flipper's quarters, Wilhelmi testified:

In the wardrobe in the back room, clothing of Lieut. Flipper and his servant was all mixed up. Her skirt was hanging over a pair of pants, or a pair of pants under a skirt and a coat over a skirt—there were three pieces of clothing on the same hook. Hair brushes and combs were on the wash stand which were claimed by the servant of Lieutenant Flipper. An old tooth brush and an old comb was there, and also some bedding on the bed which she claimed belonged to her. A sewing machine was back there. It was near the bed in the main quarters.[11]

In searching Flipper himself, Wilhelmi said he and Edmunds asked him to turn out his pockets.

The first pocket that we examined was the pocket on the right hand side of his blouse. He pulled out a hand-kerchief and at the same time a check flew out which had been on the top of the handkerchief—of $56.00. . . . It was a check which I had given him on the tenth of August. It was a personal check for my commissary bill for July, that of the band and the post bakery.[12]

Barber began cross-examining Wilhelmi by bringing up the circular to the Mexicans, asked them to bring burros to the post, so that officers and soldiers could race them for prizes. It developed that the race had been organized by two other officers, who had asked Flipper to prepare notices in Spanish since he spoke the language, and that Wilhelmi himself had been among the many officers who contributed prize money.[13]

Reviewing Shafter's orders to bring Flipper in from town, Barber asked if the colonel specifically expressed fears that he might leave the country.

"I think it was after the arrest of Lieutenant Flipper that Colonel Shafter said it would have been an easy matter of Lieutenant Flipper to have gone to Mexico," Wilhelmi said.

"When you returned from bringing Mr. Flipper back did you say anything to Colonel Shafter about the idea of Mr. Flipper escaping to Mexico?" Barber asked Wilhelmi.

"I think not."

"Before starting to go for Mr. Flipper did you or not, and since your report to Colonel Shafter after your return, have you not talked with him on the subject?"

Why should you, the gentlemen of the court, sit here and permit this accused in court to verify this list? Why can't he step up like a man to his commanding officer and ask for his property? . . . Was he not offered the property twice? No inventory would have been necessary, had he taken the property at the time when it was offered to him. This court would never had been troubled with the subject.

Clous added that in a civil proceeding, "This subject would have been kicked out of court," and went on to question Barber's motive for bringing it up.[21]

Barber replied that he had no ulterior motive.

Everything connected with this case is proper to come before this court. What is the penalty for embezzlement? Fine and imprisonment. How much fine has he already paid? Where is the property? . . . We could have been half way through with the testimony by this time. It looks to me as if the judge-advocate is laboring under a terrible state of mind, that something terrible is going to take place at some other time.[22]

After more arguments, the court overruled Clous and allowed the examination. Once the property was examined and verified, the court was closed. When it reconvened in open session, Clous announced he had been directed to return the property to the custody of Wilhelmi and Shafter.[23] Cross-examination continued, with Wilhelmi testifying that others besides himself, Edmunds, and Flipper were present during the initial search, adding:

I don't know who it was. [I] know it was a Mexican and I told him to get out of there. . . . [T]hey came in while we were there. There were one or two others in the back room. While we examined the back room the Mexican came into the front room, but he was in my sight all the time, and he did not take anything while we were there or touch anything. I took particular care to observe him in that respect.

Asked if the Mexican and Flipper had spoken to each other, Wilhelmi replied, "I think there was something said—just a few words. . . . It was in Mexican and I did not understand it. I can't tell what it was."[24]

As Wilhelmi continued, it became obvious that during the search, several persons were milling about the back room of Flipper's quarters. Neither Wilhelmi nor Edmunds appears to have made any effort to note who they were or what they were doing or to otherwise control them, but allowed them to come and go as they pleased. In fact, Wilhelmi was not even certain whether they were Mexican or black, or whether Lucy Smith was among them. He indicated Flipper had divided his time between talking with the visitors and assisting in the search.[25]

Now Barber turned to Wilhelmi's brief career at West Point, in an apparent effort to show he resented Flipper's success at the academy, compared to his own failure to graduate. Wilhelmi testified he first saw Flipper at West Point in June 1873. This drew an immediate objection from Clous on grounds of relevancy and materiality.

Barber replied that he had the right to ask Wilhelmi anything about his personal life or his relations with Flipper, and the objection was overruled. Wilhelmi said originally he had been in the class ahead of Flipper but was turned back to Flipper's class and remained in that class from June 1, 1873, until his health forced him to resign from the academy in December of that year. During that period, he did not know Flipper personally, nor did he have the opportunity to speak with him.

"How long were you at the Point while Mr. Flipper was there?" Barber asked. Clous objected again, and continued to object as Barber withdrew or rephrased the questions. When Clous objected to Barber's asking what Wilhelmi did after he resigned, Barber insisted on the question and was upheld. Wilhelmi replied that he moved to Philadelphia and, after regaining his health, went into the insurance business, which he practiced until he entered the army on October 15, 1875.[26]

"After you left the Point and up to the time that you were appointed to the army, were you at any time engaged in any detective business?" Barber then asked.

Wilhelmi replied that he was not, nor had he ever been involved in any "business of a detective character."

"This matter was your first experience?"

"Which matter?" Wilhelmi asked.

"This matter with Lieutenant Flipper."

Clous objected, and Barber withdrew the question with the comment, "I hope the judge advocate will not scold me any more than he can help and not take up the time of the court."

"I am not scolding," Clous groused. "I am simply attending to my duty, and I am responsible to no one here for it, least of all, the gentleman who represents the defense."

Winding up the cross-examination, Barber ascertained Wilhelmi's first encounter with Flipper after leaving West Point was in March 1881, when Wilhelmi was transferred with Shafter's staff to Fort Davis. Wilhelmi described his subsequent relations with Flipper as "friendly." Asked to define "friendly," he explained that while he and Flipper never visited each other socially, their working relationship was more cordial than the perfunctory formality required of officers in an official capacity.[27] With that, Barber announced that his cross-examination was finished.

Under examination by Clous, Wilhelmi recalled a conversation with Flipper in the guardhouse after his arrest, in which they had discussed the falsified reports. According to Wilhelmi, Flipper explained why he had lied to Shafter by saying, "Well, you know how the colonel is, an erratic sort of man, and when he ordered me on the eighth of July to send the money off, I reported it so on the ninth."[28]

For the most part, Barber's cross-examination of Wilhelmi was little more than a smoke screen. Clous had been absolutely right in suspecting his motives for bringing up the matter of personal property, as Flipper had already been offered its return. It was nothing more than an effort to convince the court that Flipper had been subjected to unwarranted harassment. He tried—and failed—to establish a grudge because Flipper had graduated from the academy, whereas Wilhelmi's health had forced him to resign. Yet, what was the point? Wilhelmi was still an army officer, and post and regimental adjutant. And it would not have impressed the members of the court, none of whom, as previously stated, were themselves West Pointers. Finally, Barber attempted to establish that Wilhelmi had functioned as a bungling detective, when, in fact, he was investigating nothing; he simply was searching Flipper's quarters for missing funds, under orders issued by the commanding officer, and well within his responsibilities as post adjutant.

On the other hand, Barber had scored one major point. He had shown that the search was haphazard and sloppy. No effort had been made to keep others out of Flipper's quarters while the search was under way. In fact, Wilhelmi had given so little attention to them that he could not even recall their race, much less who they were.

The final point, however, went to Clous. In his closing reexamination of Wilhelmi, he had bolstered the charge that Flipper had lied to his commanding officer. Flipper never disputed this under oath, and even years later, he would tacitly admit to it.

7

THE GOVERNMENT RESTS

Finished, for the most part, with Wilhelmi as a witness, Judge Advocate Clous called Lieutenant Edmunds Edmunds testified that when he went to relieve Flipper of his commissary duties, he found a large amount of money "piled indiscriminately on his desk, currency and silver . . . [in] no regular order."[1] During the subsequent search that led to Flipper's arrest, he said he and Wilhelmi found "considerable money in the desk scattered around in different places, a great many private papers were in the desk, letters and other papers."[2]

After finding cash scattered haphazardly elsewhere throughout the quarters, Edmunds said he had told Flipper, "Good gracious, you don't keep all this money in your quarters, do you?" Flipper replied that he did.[3]

Clous continued to elicit testimony that simply backed what Shafter and Wilhelmi already had said. Then, in a shift of tack, he introduced into evidence a letter from Flipper to Wilhelmi in the latter's capacity as adjutant, dated August

17, asking for the return of Mexican currency and personal effects that had been taken during the various searches of his quarters.

In that letter, Flipper said the Mexican money "has been in my possession for a long time as curiosities and it is my wish to preserve them." He indicated he expected return of his personal property once the deficit had been covered, and defined the property as "my jewelry of every sort and description. I do not refer to papers of any kind." This was the application previously mentioned in Colonel Shafter's testimony, and which the colonel had endorsed.[4]

Given Clous's continual prior insistence that Flipper's property would be returned to him on application, that the application had, in fact, been made three months previously, and that the property was still in the possession of Shafter and Wilhelmi, it is incredible that Barber let the matter pass. In *Flipper's Dismissal*, Barry C. Johnson reminds the reader that Barber and Flipper already had allowed the property to be brought into court, examined, and then returned to Shafter without a word of protest. As Johnson says, "The suspicion is difficult to avoid that it suited the Defense to leave this property at post headquarters, as a 'grudge' against Shafter and Wilhelmi."[5] In short, both sides were playing games.

The letter was a prelude to Clous's introduction of Flipper's weekly statements for May, which he said were examples of testimony drawn out during cross-examination by the defense.[6] Barber replied that his cross-examination did not bring out these statements, but that Clous himself had done it in his examinations of Shafter, Wilhelmi, and Edmunds. Barber detailed the charges and specifications against Flipper, pointing out that while they were based on allegations of misconduct in July and August, Clous was reaching back into statements from a prior month. "They have no right to come before the court as illustrative of testimony—they illustrate nothing," he concluded.

Addressing Colonel Pennypacker and the court, Clous said, "Mr. President, it is very refreshing, very amusing to me that the counsel for the defense has at last sought refuge in the charges and specifications before this court. For a week or more past, he has not looked at them, I don't think, when he entered the cross-examination of this case." The papers, he said, were to lead into testimony as to Flipper's intentions, something he felt the government had every right to do.[7]

"Why don't you bring his horse into court?" Barber asked. "It might with just as much propriety come in here, according to the testimony of Lieutenant Wilhelmi." The court was unimpressed with that bit of sarcasm, and after deliberation in closed session, it overruled Barber's objection.[8]

Clous's real point for bringing up the statements came out during reexamination. He intended to prove that the deficiency dated back as far as May, and that in order to conceal that deficiency, some weekly statements for May had been erased. These statements, he said, were not forwarded, nor were statements for June or July. "I shall attempt to show you that there was a studied attempt on the part of the accused to deceive his commanding officer from May on to July as to the real amount of funds he was responsible for."[9]

Now the government's strategy was out in the open, and Barber could only reiterate his objection that there was nothing in the charges and specifications concerning funds in May. Once again, he was overruled.[10]

Clous showed the statements to Edmunds and asked if they were in the same condition as they had been found in Flipper's quarters. The witness replied they were not, indicating the original entries had been made in ink and these had been erased. After recovering the statements, Edmunds explained he had checked them against the cash books in the commissary office, and noted the differences in pencil next to the erasures. Some additional notations had been made in pencil, apparently by Colonel Shafter.[11]

Barber entered another objection, and Clous seized the opportunity to speculate on the defense's own line of questioning. "Since my attention has been drawn to the statement for June," Clous began, "I will make one further remark. Is it not plausible to presume . . . that these weekly statements for June were never presented to any commanding officer, that having made so many erasures in May that the matter could not be continued all the time without attracting attention?"

If that were the case, Clous asked, wasn't it possible that Flipper made two sets of statements, one with erasures to cover his mistakes, and one clean? The clean copies would have been presented for Shafter's signature. The erased copies, without Shafter's signature, were presented in court in an effort by the defense to show the colonel had never checked the statements for June, and was therefore himself negligent.[12] Yet, without evidence that two separate statements were made, Clous could do nothing more than speculate, and the court did not appear interested.

Barber's cross-examination was similar to his questioning of Wilhelmi. He determined that Edmunds had been Flipper's French instructor at West Point from about September 1873 until February 1875, but they had not met again until May 1881 at Fort Davis. Until the time of the arrest, Edmunds said he considered Flipper's character to be "above reproach."[13]

Bringing up the "Mexican theory" again, Barber asked Edmunds if, on the night he relieved Flipper, he had noticed anything about the latter's dress, appearance, or manners or anything in his quarters that might be suspicious.

"No, sir," Edmunds replied, "I can't say there was. Simply the large amount of money that was there. That attracted my attention and that was the only thing that did."[14]

Discussing the search, Edmunds said he told Flipper that all his personal effects would be returned to him except his watch, which Colonel Shafter was keeping to secure a loan. Shafter soon offered to return the watch as well, saying he did not want Flipper to feel pressed to repay the money. Flipper, however, declined to accept any property before consulting his attorney or except through civil authorities.[15]

After Edmunds, Captain Bates testified that he had signed Flipper's weekly statements any time Shafter was absent.[16] That being the only question for Bates, Commissary Sgt. Carl Ross was called. He identified various statements he had prepared but noticed erasures on several of them. He also produced a copy book showing the original amounts.[17]

The questioning of Sergeant Ross was completed on November 25, and the bulk of it simply restated what the court had heard before. He did point out, however, that the commissary office had a secure safe. Rather than placing the checks in that safe, however, Flipper had them in his possession when he left the office.[18] Clous would remind the court of this during his closing arguments.

Another point of Ross's testimony also was significant. He testified that he made up the letter of transmittal for funds on August 10 but that Flipper did not sign it until August 11, after his quarters were searched.[19]

The following day, after Ross had a chance to hear his testimony read back, Clous announced he had no further testimony. Although Shafter's testimony had been left open to recall, he said he did not believe it was necessary. Barber, however, felt it was necessary, and Shafter again took the stand.

"Did you not during the occurrence of these events which you have narrated in your testimony, or since their occurrence, have you not expressed animosity toward Lieutenant Flipper, or used harsh and threatening language toward Lieutenant Flipper?" Barber asked.

"I don't think that I ever made any expressions showing animosity against Mr. Flipper until since the publication of a letter long since his arrest that appeared in a New York paper that contained two or three—one falsehood and some aspersions upon me personally," Shafter replied, adding, "Since then I in speaking with other people perhaps used harsh expressions but never before that, that I know of."

"That is all," Barber said.

But after the statement was read back by the clerk, Shafter commented, "I will add to that, that I don't think I have ever used any threatening language in reference to Lieutenant Flipper in regard to this case which is being tried, or that I have ever expressed any animosity toward him other than to say that I thought I had been deceived in his character, and had no sympathy for him since the publication of that letter."

"That is all," Barber repeated, with which Shafter stepped down, and Clous announced, "The prosecution now rests."[20]

The Quarles letter had come home to roost.

8

LUCY SMITH TESTIFIES

The Flipper affair had briefly captured national attention but was now becoming old news, because a far more important case was under way elsewhere. In Washington, Charles Guiteau was on trial for the murder of President James A. Garfield, and the scene in that courtroom, with a half-mad defendant, made far more interesting reading than the mundane recitation of financial affairs at Fort Davis. Regarding the latter, the *San Antonio Daily Express* reported: "The defense in the Flipper case commenced offering their testimony . . . and seven witnesses were rapidly examined, and at this date [November 30] it will soon bring the trial to a close."

Indeed, even Merritt Barber was surprised at how quickly the trial was now moving.[1] When Clous bothered to cross-examine at all, his questions were perfunctory.

Lieutenant S. L. Woodward answered a few questions on the transfer of funds from Fort Quitman, which was supplied as a subpost of Fort Davis. Captain Bates, now called as a defense witness, said that he and Capt. C. D. Vielé had organized the burro race covered in Wilhelmi's testimony and that Flipper had been asked to assist. When his turn came, Vielé could not remember any details concerning the organization of the race, only that Flipper had assisted him in forming the starting line, "because I could not make those Mexicans understand me." He also testified that he had noticed Flipper's horse saddled, with bags attached, "a day or two before the arrest." He indicated he had paid particular attention because the saddle was the Whitman pattern, rather than the standard issue McClellan, and Vielé had only recently ordered one himself. When he asked if the bags came with the saddle, Flipper replied they were custom made.[2]

The saddlebags, which Shafter had taken as an indication Flipper might flee into Mexico, were covered at length by the next witness, Walter David Cox, who had been Flipper's orderly and tended his horse since the previous February 1. Cox said that Flipper customarily carried the bags attached to his saddle, and that during the entire period since February removed them only once, when they were repaired by the company saddler. He also testified that the bags were empty when he saddled Flipper's horse and took it to him on the day Shafter ordered him back on post.[3]

Fort Davis merchants J. B. Shields and A. W. Keesey, both of whom had loaned money to cover Flipper's deficit, testified as character witnesses. Shields, who contributed fifty dollars, said he knew "plenty of other citizens who would have contributed, but it happened at a very dull time, when very few except the storekeepers had any money to contribute." Asked his reasons for helping Flipper, Shields said:

> The first was because I believed he was innocent of what he was charged with. The next was I thought he was rather crowded [in the guardhouse] and that it was a pretty hard place for an officer or any other man

to be in a cell closed up, and from his intelligence and good behavior, I liked the man and tried to help him if I could.[4]

Under cross-examination by Clous, Shields acknowledged that during a food shortage the previous spring, Flipper had provided him with food for his family, but he understood it was Flipper's personal mess rather than from commissary stores.[5]

Keesey testified he had provided two hundred dollars for Flipper's deficit, although it left him short of needed cash. He also said he had advanced goods to the post commissary, not only under Flipper but under every commissary officer at Fort Davis for the previous eighteen months to two years. He was reimbursed goods when the commissary was resupplied by the army, although, he was quick to point out, he never quite broke even. Keesey added he met frequently with Flipper and vouched for his integrity as a man who did not gamble or indulge in "habits of disipation [sic]."[6]

Court adjourned three days until 11 A.M. November 29.[7] Then, after covering procedural matters from the previous session, Barber called the witness who undoubtedly excited the most curiosity: Lucy Smith.

Little, if anything, is known about Lucy's background. She may have been married (during the trial, she often was referred to as Mrs. Smith); even so, it was obvious to all that she was Flipper's mistress as well as his housekeeper. In Victorian fashion, the relationship was skirted throughout the proceedings, although at one point Clous pointedly credited himself with an effort to avoid "bringing any scandal in the case."[8] The implications, however, were too much to the contrary. During his initial testimony, Shafter referred to her as "Lucy Flipper," although he immediately amended it to "Smith."[9] Even Barber, during his examination, referred to the time that she had "lived" with Flipper, and she made no effort to correct him.[10] This obvious relationship flaunted deeply entrenched Victorian values that dictated if such a relationship even existed (and ideally it would not), it should be at least discreet. Besides the moral code of society as a whole, the caste system at posts like Fort Davis separated people not only by race but by class. The system was reinforced on the frontier where, removed from the mainstream of society, the residents of Officers' Row strove all the more to preserve, outwardly at least, what they perceived as the values of that society. Officers and their wives often lived in a sort of fantasy world where, as Oliver Knight observed in his social society of the frontier army, the officer was expected to be a cavalier *sans peur et sans reproche* (a favorite expression of the era, as Knight points out). They were expected to socialize only with each other or with civilians of equal status and to avoid enlisted or serving personnel except when necessity required. The arrangement between Flipper and Lucy, although of the same race, violated social convention.[11]

Free on personal recognizance pending her own trial in federal district court, and with Flipper's court-martial under way, Lucy acknowledged that she still cooked, washed, and ironed for him.[12] Except for a trip to Fort Stockton in the spring, she claimed that prior to Flipper's arrest she had roomed with a Mrs. Olsup, presumably in town. While living with Mrs. Olsup, she kept her personal belongings in a trunk in a tent, which she indicated was pitched outside Flipper's quarters. She also kept some of her belongings in a trunk in Flipper's front room and in a chest in the hallway, "because I had no room, I had no place to put my things for safety and I asked him if I could not keep them in his trunk." Flipper kept the trunk locked and when she wanted the keys, she had to ask for them.[13]

So far so good. Now, however, Lucy went into memory lapses and began suffering from a severe case of "fright." The further into the questioning, the more frequent the two phenomena became. To begin with, she could not remember what happened the morning of Flipper's arrest. Under continued questioning from Barber, she did recall that she was doing the laundry and had asked for the keys to the trunk so that she could put his clothing away and get some of hers.

"Did you take out any papers and envelopes?" Barber asked.

"I taken out two envelopes. . . . I put them in my bosom."

"What was the cause of your taking out the envelopes?"

"Because I was in this trunk and I had taken some things out, and because I had a woman in there working that was not very honest," she replied.[14]

Why Lucy did not simply lock the trunk with the envelopes still inside was not explored by either side. It does, however, raise the question of who really might have been the dishonest woman in Flipper's quarters. Equally interesting is that no one bothered to ask Lucy to name the "woman in there."

Asked if Flipper had given her any instructions with the keys, Lucy replied, "He said, 'Lucy, don't go away and leave that trunk open, be very careful and keep it locked when you go away and when you go away give me back the keys.' That is what he always told me . . . in going away when I had the trunk open, to be sure to lock it up and hand him the keys and when I went out, to lock the doors." She said Flipper never discussed the reason, and did not mention to her anything about the papers on that particular morning.

"Then, if I understand you," Barber said, "you took them out without his knowledge?"

Answering affirmatively, she then said when she put the clothes away, she laid the keys on the table, since she had not finished with his laundry. She could not remember whether she had locked the trunk.

Although, after the initial memory lapse, Lucy seemed to have remarkable recall, the lapses now became very pronounced, and she became especially frightened at the mention of Colonel Shafter. She told Barber that she did not remember where she had gone after she had taken the envelopes. "I was cleaning up," she said. "I was around the house."

"You remember Colonel Shafter coming there?"

"I don't remember anything about it."

"Did you see Colonel Shafter that morning?" Barber pressed.

"I don't remember whether I seen him or not. I was so scared."

"Do you remember Colonel Shafter coming there to the kitchen and speaking to you—did you go over to Colonel Shafter's office?"

"I don't remember whether I went over there or not. I was scared to death," Lucy insisted.

"Where did you go during that day?"

"I went to jail for one place," she said.

"Where were you when you were taken to the jail? Where did you go from?" Barber asked.

"I don't know, Captain, because I was so scared, I don't know where I was taken from."

"What scared you?"

"I can't tell you that," Lucy said. "I don't know what scared me. I was scared though."[15]

Perhaps to give Lucy some breathing space—or perhaps to try the extent of her sporadic amnesia—Barber asked an irrelevant question about a ring Flipper had given her. When she answered that in detail, he asked if she remembered what had happened to the envelopes she had taken from Flipper's trunk. Once again, she remembered absolutely nothing.[16]

Under cross-examination from Clous, she no longer remembered even being arrested, saying instead, "I kind of remember I was in jail." Nor did she recall being examined by U.S. Commissioner Hartnett.[17]

"When you saw Colonel Shafter, did not he ask you whether you had any papers about you, and did not you

answer him [that[you did not have anything about you?"
Clous asked.

"I don't remember anything about it for I was frightened
to death. That is the way of it," Lucy answered.

"You don't remember having said so on that occasion and
locality?"

"No, sir. I don't remember anything about it, because I
ain't got over my scare yet."[18]

In question after question, she repeated that she was too
frightened to remember. She did not remember anything
about the hearing before Hartnett. She did not remember
telling a soldier that nothing could happen to Flipper because
she "had it fixed all right." She did not recognize the
envelopes that were taken from her. As for anything she
might have said to Shafter, "If I said it, I ain't responsible for
it because I was frightened to death. . . . The very sights of
Colonel Shafter frightened me. . . . The sights of Colonel
Shafter scares me near to death."[19]

One can imagine that Lucy would have been frightened.
She was a black woman in trouble with the white man's law.
It is more than likely, also, that she knew a great deal about
the missing money, which would have aggravated her fears.
Either way, it certainly would have been traumatic for her.
On the other hand, Shafter had also suffered from convenient
attacks of forgetfulness any time something came up that
might make him look culpable. Lucy had a much better
chance of doing the same and getting away with it; given the
racial stereotypes of the time, the sight of a frightened, confused black woman appeared to raise no suspicions among
the white officers of the court or the two white attorneys. No
one thought to press her on contradictory memory lapses
covering a period of several days. No one pressed her to try to
remember at least something of her search by Shafter, her
arrest, her incarceration, her statement before Hartnett, and
the filing of federal charges against her.

At one point during cross-examination, Clous asked Lucy if she had dressed herself in Flipper's quarters, and she answered no. Picking up on that in reexamination, Barber asked if she slept or had ever spent the night in Flippers quarters.

"No, sir," she replied. "I went to a dance once and after I came home Mrs. Olsup and I went into the kitchen and staid [there] all night because we danced to three o'clock. Mr. Flipper did not know I was on the place."

"That was the only time you was [sic] there. . . . And Mrs. Olsup was with you?"

"Yes, sir."[20]

In the end, neither Barber nor Clous gained anything substantial from Lucy Smith. In allowing her confusion and memory lapses to go unchallenged, the court committed what probably was its only error during the entire trial. Her testimony—essentially useless to either side—was allowed to stand. If Flipper had depended on her to help, or if Clous had hoped to use her against him, both were sorely mistaken.

When Lucy was finished, one more witness, Joseph Sender, took the stand before adjournment for the day. It was Sender's mercantile establishment Flipper was visiting when Wilhelmi went to bring him back to the post. Sender's appearance as a character witness is significant to posterity primarily because of an incident illustrating the attitudes of the period. Before administering the oath, Clous asked if Sender, as an "Israelite," considered it binding. Upon answering affirmatively, Sender was sworn in and testified that his firm had contributed five hundred dollars to cover Flipper's deficit, which was charged to Flipper on the company books.[21]

9

TESTIMONIALS
TO A GOOD NAME

"F un For Flipper" was the *San Antonio Daily Express's* headline as a parade of witnesses marched through to testify to the defendant's character.[1] Pride and institutional necessity made character an integral part of military tribunals. "Courts-martial will always allow prisoners to produce evidence as to character," the contemporary *Treatise on Military Law* noted, adding, "in fact, the members often advise a soldier to produce such evidence." Such testimony was particularly important in Flipper's case because of the charge of embezzlement. The *Treatise* elaborated, saying, "Where *intent* is the principal ingredient in the charge, or where circumstantial proof only is adduced, evidence as to character, *bearing on the charge,* may be highly important." In the embezzlement charge, the government's case was entirely circumstantial.[2]

Barber accelerated his effort to establish Flipper's good name by calling W. S. Chamberlain, a watchmaker at Fort Davis, who was boarding with Flipper at the time of his arrest. It was Chamberlain who had gone to the other merchants and citizens of the town and raised the money to cover Flipper's deficit. He probably was closer to Flipper than any other witness except Lucy, and now Barber hoped he would fill in some of the gaps in testimony up to that point.

Chamberlain testified that he had heard Flipper caution Lucy about the security of his room and papers "very frequently." He added he remembered that after breakfast on the morning of Flipper's arrest, they were in the front room when Lucy asked him for something. Flipper withdrew the article from his pocket and gave it to her, although Chamberlain could not be certain whether it was the key to his trunk.[3]

Shortly afterward, Chamberlain went to his shop, where he later learned Flipper had been arrested. Because he understood Flipper was being held incommunicado, Chamberlain did not see him again until he visited him in the guardhouse the following Monday. After discussing the case with Flipper, Chamberlain went to headquarters to see if reimbursement of the money might help. He remembered Shafter as saying, "Yes, it will save him from the penitentiary. . . . I will buck up a hundred dollars myself."[4]

Chamberlain testified that within a couple of days, he and Sender had covered the amount in cash and due bills, thus satisfying Shafter. During that conversation, the colonel told them "he always thought Lieutenant Flipper to be an honest man, and did not believe that he was guilty, that there was some one else to the bottom of it. . . . I think his remark was that there was some 'damned nigger' at the bottom of it."[5]

Chamberlain added he considered Flipper reasonably frugal, allowing himself "a dollar or two dollars" each week to attend Mexican *bailes*, but generally living within his means.[6]

The penultimate witness for the defense was Fort Davis attorney J. M. Dean, who had represented Lucy Smith during her hearing before Commissioner Hartnett. After Lucy's hearing, Dean said he overheard Shafter remark "he would get Flipper or that he was on his trail, or made some remark of that sort, that he was getting more evidence on him."

"Did he say anything about piling it up on him?" Barker asked.

"Yes, sir, he said he was piling it up on him. . . . I had been led to believe that Colonel Shafter was acting as the friend of Lieutenant Flipper and was disposed to act square towards him, but after I heard him make that remark I came to the conclusion that he was playing him double."[7]

Actually, there was no intentional duplicity in Shafter's attitude. It was simply part of the colonel's suspicious and unforgiving nature. He had trusted Flipper and believed him innocent. Given the isolation of many frontier military posts, shortage of ready cash, the tendency to handle transactions by credit or check pending the irregular arrival of the paymaster, and the uncertainty of monetary transfers to a distant departmental headquarters, disorder in the commissary funds was not unusual. Flipper, however, had lied about the transmission of funds to San Antonio and had tried to cover his losses with a check he knew to be worthless. This, in Shafter's view, was bad enough. The real outrage came, however, after Flipper attacked the colonel's character in the letter to Quarles, which appeared in the national press. Deceived and publicly insulted by a very junior officer, Shafter now believed Flipper capable of anything, and let his imagination run wild. Then, having convinced himself that Flipper was a villain of the deepest dye, he set about to prove it.[8]

Meanwhile, Dean testified that Flipper initially had confidence in Shafter, and felt the colonel was working toward clearing him of suspicion. Visiting Flipper to get information for Lucy's habeas corpus petition, Dean said:

> He led me to believe that he thought Colonel Shafter was his friend, and I told him that . . . from what I had heard Colonel Shafter say, that I thought it would be to his interest to conduct this matter without Colonel Shafter's assistance . . . that I had never heard Colonel Shafter say anything in Flipper's behalf, but on the other hand had been against him.[9]

After Dean, Maj. N. B. McLaughlin, the former post commander, testified to Flipper's upstanding character and performance as a soldier. This was as close as Flipper would come to the recommendation in *Treatise on Military Law* that "[t]he most proper person to call for [as a character witness], generally speaking, will be the prisoner's commanding officer."[10] Nevertheless, McLaughlin's testimony, free of the rancor that tainted relations between Flipper and Shafter, undoubtedly helped.

Barber had no more witnesses, but he asked to enter a letter from Colonel Grierson as Flipper's regimental commander. Clous objected, saying he understood that if Grierson were present, he would testify to Flipper's character. However, the judge advocate did not consider any portion of the letter pertaining to the case as being proper evidence.[11]

The letter, which was then read for the court's consideration, stated that until his arrest, Flipper's

> veracity and integrity, have never been questioned and his character and standing, as an officer and a gentleman, have certainly been beyond reproach. He came under my immediate command in 1880, during the Campaign against Victorio's band of hostile Indians, and from personal observation, I can testify to his efficiency and gallantry in the field.
>
> General Davidson [John W. Davidson, Flipper's commanding officer at Fort Sill], Captain Nolan and others under whom he has served, have spoken of him to me in the highest terms, and he has repeatedly been selected for special and important duties, and discharged them faithfully and in a highly satisfactory manner. Being, as an officer, the only representative of his race in the Army, he has, under circumstances and surroundings the most unfavorable and discouraging, steadily won his way by sterling worth and ability, by manly and soldierly bearing, to the confidence, respect and esteem of all with whom he has served or come in contact.

As to Lieutenant Flipper's late trouble or alleged offence for which he is now being Court-martialed, I have no personal knowledge, but from all information I have been able to gain relative thereto—although he may have committed irregularities, from want of experience,—my confidence in his honesty of purpose has not been shaken, and my faith in his final vindication is still as strong as ever. . . . I, as his Colonel,—believing that his restoration to duty would give great satisfaction to the regiment—most heartily and earnestly commend him to the leniency of the Court and reviewing authorities.[12]

After hearing the letter, the court overruled Clous on the grounds that Barber was submitting it as a testimonial to Flipper's character, rather than as evidence.[13]

Grierson's letter is interesting. To begin with, it was dated November 1, before testimony even began. One may surmise that Barber had been sitting on it for at least three weeks. It also contained the phrase "most heartily and earnestly commend him to the leniency of the Court and reviewing authorities." In other words, from the beginning, Grierson apparently anticipated a guilty verdict. Otherwise, Flipper would not need the leniency of the court or a reviewing authority. Grierson's preference for writing a letter, rather than filing a sworn affidavit or appearing in person to offer sworn testimony as a character witness, likewise is noteworthy. How much impact these factors had on the court's deliberations over the verdict will never be known.

The time had come for Flipper's statement to the court. Because of the length and complexity of the trial, court remained adjourned until December 6, to allow him sufficient opportunity to prepare it.[14]

10

THE QUESTION: CAN AN OFFICER BE BLACK?

The trial was in its twenty-eighth day when Flipper finally spoke. Rather than testify and refute the allegations of Shafter and others under oath, he read a prepared statement, which set the tone of his later appeals.

> I declare to you in the most solemn and impressive manner possible that I am perfectly innocent in every manner, shape or form, that I have never myself nor by another appropriated, converted or applied to my own use a single dollar or a single penny of the money of the government or permitted it to be done, or authorized any meddling with it whatever. Of *crime* I am *not* guilty. The funds for which I was responsible I kept in my own quarters in my trunk.... My reasons for keeping them there were that as I was responsible for their safety I felt more secure to have them in my own personal custody....

Discussing Lucy Smith's access to his trunk, he continued:

I had no reason to question the honesty of any of the persons about my house as I had never missed anything that attracted my attention, and when the officers searched that trunk and failed to find the funds which I had put in there three days before[,] I was perfectly astounded and could hardly believe the evidence of my own senses. As to where that money went or who took it I am totally ignorant.

Defending himself against the second charge, he reviewed the lapse in reporting brought about by Small's absence from San Antonio during May:

Sometime in May the actual cash on hand did not meet the amount for which I was responsible. I was owing a considerable bill myself which it was not convenient to pay, and as there was a large amount due me from men and laundresses, I believed that my shortage was accounted for in that way, but as the funds were not to be transmitted for some time it did not occasion me any uneasiness, as I felt confident of getting it in by the time it would be required.

He recounted his trouble in obtaining checks and his false hopes that he could make up the amount by collecting from companies coming in from the field. He also mentioned Small's second absence from San Antonio, which led him to believe he could make up the balance with the $1,440 check, which he thought would be covered by royalties from his publisher.

On the morning of the 10th of August, I took what checks I had to the commissary sergeant and directed him to make a letter of transmittal of them and directed him to . . . search for checks to meet the money I had, expecting daily a deposit from Homer Lee & Co., but there were no checks to be procured and no deposit was made. On the 13th of August when I left my house with Mr. Chamberlain I have every reason to believe and do believe that all the funds for which I was responsible was [sic] in the trunk and in my quarters except for the $1440 which I have already explained, and the amount of my commissary bill for July which I had not paid. As to their disappearance I have no privity or knowledge and am not responsible except to make the amount good, and that I have done.

As to my motives in the matter alleged in the first specification of the second charge I can only say that some time before I had been cautioned that the commanding officer would improve any opportunity to get me into trouble, and although I did not give much credit to it at the time, it occurred to me very prominently when I found myself in difficulty; and as he had long been known to me by reputation and observation as a severe, stern man, having committed my first mistake I indulged what proved to be a false hope that I would be able to work out my responsibilities alone and avoid giving him any knowledge of my embarrassment.[1]

The assertion that Shafter had previously been searching for a means by which he might "improve any opportunity" to make trouble for Flipper is unsubstantiated by the record. Despite Shafter's definite racial bias, the evidence indicates that when the problem first arose, he was more interested in preserving Flipper's integrity as an army officer than persecuting him as a black officer. Flipper may have feared Shafter's reaction to his mismanagement—indeed he had reason to. Yet one of the defense's own witnesses had testified that Flipper, in the guardhouse, still believed Shafter would try to help him. This is hardly the attitude of a man who previously had been cautioned to be careful of entrapment by his commanding officer.

After Flipper finished, Barber began his summation. Flipper, he said,

is struggling for his crown; for the spotless record of
nine long years, and he could not do otherwise than
fight the battle inch by inch and steel to steel. . . .
Regarding his pleas and testimony together you will
observe that the accused does not present his action
under the second charge [conduct unbecoming an
officer and a gentleman] as blameless, but he presents
it just as it is, placing before you as nearly as he can
his faults and his motives and asks that they be
weighed together. The first charge and its specifications [embezzlement] the accused denies *in toto* . . .
he confidently challenges the prosecution *and the
world* to show it or even the shadow of such an act.[2]

Barber then proceeded to demolish all the theories of
embezzlement, point by point. Shafter, he said, insisted that
he had verified the funds.

He knows he did it because he was here and ought to
have done it. . . . And yet all along his testimony there
are some of the most remarkable instances of forgetfulness. He forgets after signing weekly statements
of funds that they are his own papers [as post com-
mander] and that he ought to hand them to his adjutant to forward them to their destination. If he *had*
done so, if he had not forgotten his duty, would we all
have spent this long weary month at Fort Davis? For
how much of this matter is *his* forgetfulness and neglect responsible[?][3]

Shafter forgot whether he had examined the papers Wilhelmi took from Flipper's quarters, Barber said. He "forgot
that he had ordered [Lucy Smith] stripped until he saw we
intended to show it." He forgot his affidavit before Commissioner Hartnett, Barber continued, and he could not remember his testimony before the commissioner.

And finally ends up with the general proposition that he does not recollect *trifling* events, but only the *important* items pertaining to the command of the post. Is the weekly verification of funds one of those important items that a commanding officer remembers for months, or is it a simple routine which is attended to or not as the officer submits them or not?[4]

Barber pointed out that, contrary to Shafter's fears and allegations, Flipper had not destroyed any papers that could be—and were—used as evidence against him. All the paperwork was accounted for. Only the money was short, and Flipper was as mystified as any about its disappearance.[5]

Barber then turned on Wilhelmi's testimony with its emphasis on what the defense considered irrelevancies, such as Lucy's clothing scattered around and mixed with Flipper's; the position of Flipper's saddlebags; a check Wilhelmi himself had given him a couple of days before, and which Flipper apparently had stuck into his pocket and forgotten. "All these little injections of gratuitous suspicions are so manifest as to justify a suspicion on *our* part of unkindness toward the accused, that he had succeeded perhaps in winning laurels at West Point of which *his* [Wilhelmi's] sickness had prevented him from obtaining."[6]

As for the government's contention that there were duplicate weekly statements, Barber said there was no "proof or probability." There was no evidence that Flipper had used government funds to pay his own bills in town. On the contrary, it was established during the trial that at least once, he had drawn an advance on pay to settle his accounts. If there was any evidence that Flipper had stolen money, the search would have uncovered some trace of it.

The mere fact of the shortage does not establish the *intent* any more than it does the conversion [of funds to his own use], and with the explanation he gives you, makes it a harmless affair and only an illustration of carelessness in keeping his accounts.[7]

You will bear in mind that the accused is not required to prove, under the 60th Article of War, that he did *not* embezzle the money, but it is for the government to prove that he *did* embezzle it, and that he *did* knowingly and wilfully misappropriate it and apply it to his own use and benefit. Have they done so? Where, when and by what testimony? There is not a syllable of proof of it.

Even Colonel Shafter admitted that after all his investigations and reflections on the case, he did not know what happened to the money, Barber said.[8]

Moving on to conduct unbecoming an officer and a gentleman, Barber attempted to elicit the potential insecurities of the board members themselves—that is, feelings often expressed in courts-martial of the period that, "There but for the grace of God go I."[9] He called the charge "a vague and indefinite quantity, the sword of Damocles suspended by a thread over the head of every officer in the army to regulate his daily walk and conversation." The article establishing the charge could be construed according to the discretion of each individual court-martial board Barber contended, such that, strictly speaking, only Jesus Christ could inhabit the earth without committing some sort of violation.

As an example of the article's arbitrary nature, Barber pointed to the case of Paymaster Reese (mentioned in the introduction to this book), who had embezzled funds over a two-year period. Reese had been convicted of embezzlement and suspended from the service for four months but was acquitted of conduct unbecoming an officer.[10] In Flipper's case, he said:

The accused has told you his error and has given you his reasons and his motives and submitted them all to your judgment, asking you to consider his error with its surroundings, his mistake with *his* surroundings, and he appeals with confidence to your charity that you will measure his offense and its palliation together.

Cutting through Barber's lengthy rhetoric, which extended into the following day, his basic points were these:

- A cavalry officer had been placed in charge of the commissary, a position for which the army had given him neither background nor training.
- That cavalry officer was black and a former slave and therefore lacked the practical life experiences that whites took for granted.
- So long as Flipper was closely supervised, he performed his duties to the satisfaction of all concerned, but that supervision had ended when Colonel Shafter took command. In failing to exercise supervision, Shafter not only failed Flipper but also failed every officer and soldier of the Tenth Cavalry at Fort Davis.

Having made these points, Barber went over the difficulties Flipper faced because of background and race.

From the time when a mere boy he stepped upon our platform and asked the privilege of competing with us for the prize of success he has had to fight the battle of life all alone. He has had no one to turn to for counsel or sympathy. Is it strange then that when he found himself in difficulties which he could not master, and confronted with a mystery which he could not solve, he should hide it in his own breast and endeavor to work out the problem alone as he had been compelled to do all the other problems of his life? Is it strange that he should withhold his confidence from his neighbors, whose relations with him had been such as not to invite that confidence, and as he saw his expectations of relief fading one by one and his embarrassments thickening around him to hold with all the more tenacity to a vague hope which is the guiding star to those who have to fight life's battles by themselves?[11]

Barber noted that every accomplishment in Flipper's life had been done alone and against odds only a black man could appreciate.[12] He pointed out that Flipper's very position as an army officer, based on the conditions of the time, was an anomaly, and his success or failure would go far in determining the future of African Americans as officers. He then issued what amounted to a challenge to the court:

The question is before you whether it is possible for a colored man to secure and hold a position as an officer of the army.[13]

11

The End of a Career

When Barber was finished, Clous gave his closing statement, which, by comparison, was brief. Recalling Flipper's assertion that he felt the money was more secure in his trunk, the judge advocate told the court:

> Gentlemen, the government provided the accused with a strong, heavy and secure safe, over which after hours a sentinel stood guard, the regulations of his department required [him] to keep his public funds in that safe, but for weeks and months on innumerable occasions he did so keep his funds, and now at this late day he comes before you, in order to make up a plausible story, to account for his deficiency, that he considered his trunk—a portable affair, kept for the joint uses of himself and his female servant, accessible at all times to both—a more secure place of deposit than a strong iron safe, a safe which it would take the joint efforts of a body of men and draft animals to remove.[1]

From that point on, Clous said, Flipper's every action was used as an excuse for the succeeding actions, and the succeeding actions were taken to conceal the preceding ones. "He cannot urge his illegal and unlawful acts as a valid defense," he argued.

Clous noted that Shafter testified he had verified weekly statements, and Bates testified he did so in Shafter's absence; there was no testimony to the contrary.[2] No doubt, Flipper's failure to testify damaged him at this point, since only he could refute under oath the testimony of Shafter and Bates. His closing statement was just that—a statement; it did not have the same validity as sworn testimony. Certainly he could not be compelled to testify, and possibly Barber advised him against it. If so, it was a mistake. His testimony under oath, even under cross-examination by Clous, might have made a favorable impression.

As stated earlier, in the nineteenth century, courts-martial involving officer defendants essentially were courts of honor. The accused, "an officer and a gentleman" by congressional commission, was tried by other officers and gentlemen who would determine whether he was, in fact, an honorable gentleman deserving continued association with other honorable gentlemen of the army. The defendant's commission carried great weight, and there was a natural tendency to lean toward the sworn testimony of an accused officer, on the assumption that he was honor-bound to tell the truth. Conversely, the submission of a statement, rather than sworn testimony, might lead the board to believe he had something to hide.[3] Clous was right. No one had refuted Shafter's and Bates's claims (given under oath) that they had examined the statements, and now it was too late. The judge advocate scored a major point, and the court may have been influenced by the fact that rather than take the stand and defy his accusers, Flipper hid behind technicalities.

The technicalities that made up Flipper's entire case were not lost on the judge advocate, who told the court:

> [T]he Defense has failed to introduce any testimony pertinent to the issues before you and has during the progress of its side of the case confined itself almost exclusively to the question of character and to the events transpiring subsequent to the time of the commission of the offenses alleged.[4]

Going over Flipper's efforts to cover his shortage, by lying to Shafter and sending false reports to San Antonio, Clous then asked the court if there was any reason to believe him when he said the money was placed in the trunk in the first place.[5]

Having raised questions about Flipper's character, Clous hit him at his two weakest points: his arrangement with Lucy Smith and his relationship with Shafter.

> The accused, like his female servant Lucy, is ignorant of what became of the funds he claimed to have had in the envelope which was by him deposited in the household trunk, and yet, gentlemen, according to the statement of the accused and his servant, they were the only persons who had had access to that trunk or possessed the keys of the same up to the time the accused was seated near that trunk when the search commenced on August thirteenth. Strange ignorance indeed? But not so strange when we consider the fact that Lucy Smith is still the accused's servant or housekeeper.

As for Shafter, Clous said, "The accused in effect tells us that having made one false entry and told one falsehood, the stern character of his commanding officer compelled him to repeat the offense."[6]

After reviewing the government's testimony, Clous made a lengthy examination of the different definitions of embezzlement under common law, U.S. civil law, and the Articles of War. Under the articles, he noted, once the prosecution has made a prima facie case of embezzlement, then the burden of proof is thrown upon the defendant, who must show that his handling of funds was justified by particular conditions; it was not the government's responsibility to show how the accused disposed of the funds.

"I claim that the prosecution by the testimony adduced has made out not only a prima facie case of embezzlement, but also a case of embezzlement under the common law definition," Clous said.[7]

Indeed, the prosecution would have had a prima facie case, assuming the case involved *constructive* embezzlement—that is, failure to produce government funds on demand. But the words of the charge, "knowingly and willfully misappropriate and misapply," denoted *actual* embezzlement, an entirely different offense. This continued to raise the cloud of doubt, thereby weakening the government's position.

Having spent the bulk of his time on embezzlement, Clous made quick work of the charge of conduct unbecoming an officer, and concluded the case for the United States.[8]

Barber then asked that exceptions raised during the trial be attached to the formal record. The exceptions, he said, would be addressed "to the authority beyond the court," specifically General Augur and others who would review the finding and uphold or set aside whatever verdict was rendered.

Clous objected and asked for a ruling. The court upheld the objection on the grounds that the exceptions already were a matter of record.

Turning to the defendant, Clous said, "Lieutenant Flipper, your presence before this court is no longer required at this time."[9]

The court then went into closed session to deliberate Flipper's fate. Upon reconvening, "having maturely considered all the evidence accrued," the court found

> the accused, Second Lieutenant Henry O. Flipper of the Tenth Regiment of U.S. Cavalry, as follows:
> Charge I.
>> Of the specification "Not Guilty"
>> Of the first charge "Not Guilty"

Flipper had been acquitted of embezzlement.

> Charge II.
>> Of the first specification "Guilty"
>> Of the second specification "Guilty"
>> Of the third specification "Guilty"
>> Of the fourth specification "Guilty"
>> Of the fifth specification "Guilty"
>
> And the court does therefore sentence him, Second Lieutenant Henry O. Flipper of the Tenth Regiment of U.S. Cavalry "to be dismissed from the service of the United States."[10]

The record does not state how long it took to reach a verdict, nor does it provide a vote. On the ten-man board, six votes were necessary to convict. A five-five tie would have acquitted. The vote was taken in reverse order, with the junior officers announcing theirs first, so they would not be influenced by the senior officers.[11] However it went, we may presume—from a letter Flipper wrote to Capt. George A. Armes, Tenth Cavalry, at Fort Stockton, while Flipper was awaiting the outcome of the review process—that the vote was not unanimous. "The gentlemen from your post who were on my court stood by me, as I believe, like true men," he told Armes. "I can never thank Captains W. and H. too much for their kindness."[12]

"Captains W. and H." could only mean Walker and Heiner. There were various ways Flipper might have formed an idea of their views. What Barry Johnson calls "winks and nods," or other gestures in court, could demonstrate some sort of sympathy or leaning. Additionally, as the review process dragged on over the next six months, there undoubtedly would have been speculation within the officer corps, and opinions would have been expressed.[13] The fact that Flipper mentioned the officers of Fort Stockton as a group may indicate some consideration by Lieutenant Colonel Wade as well.

On December 8, 1881, one day after the verdict was rendered, the court met for the last time at 10:00 A.M. After approving the proceedings of the previous day, it adjourned sine die at 12:30 P.M. [14] The court-martial of Lieutenant Henry Ossian Flipper was over. Actual court time was thirty days, during a calendar period of almost three months, a phenomenal amount of time for any court-martial during that period. Although is the long duration was due largely to Barber's lengthy arguments and rhetoric, it also reflects the determination of the court to render a fair and just verdict. The court's patience had worn thin, as in the instance when the one member interrupted proceedings and invited Barber and Flipper to definitely establish race as a factor. Yet, the fact that this officer mentioned it indicated the possibility, with all its implications, was on the minds of the members of the board. At any time, they could have cut Barber short and demanded that he adhere solely to the evidence in the case. To their credit, they did not, instead allowing him incredible leeway in defending his client.[15]

In view of the evidence presented, there really were no other verdicts the court could have rendered. For all his references to law, Clous had failed to establish deliberate misapplication or misappropriation. The money simply was missing. As Barber maintained throughout the trial, Flipper was guilty of no more than carelessness, and the government had recovered its money primarily through Flipper's good standing in the community of Fort Davis. Yet, try as he might, Barber could not excuse Flipper's conduct when Small and Shafter had called for an accounting. He had falsified reports, issued a phony check, and he had lied. Barber could hope for leniency over what he considered Flipper's peculiar circumstances, but he could do no more than hope. The case for conduct unbecoming an officer was airtight under any interpretation, and that is how the court saw it. Surely Barber must have realized this even before deliberations began. Why else would he have asked that exceptions be attached to the record submitted to the reviewing authority?

In sentencing, the court perhaps felt itself bound to the Articles of War in ordering dismissal. It could, however, recommend him to the clemency of the reviewing authorities, but this was not done. While the reasons are unknown, one may assume the board considered the seriousness of the offenses. The crux of the Flipper affair, as Kinevan notes, was the fact that he lied in an official capacity, "and the army cannot tolerate a lack of veracity in an officer."[16] The 106th Article of War states, however, "In time of peace no sentencing of a Court Martial directing the dismissal of an officer shall be carried into execution until it should have been confirmed by the President."[17] It is charitable to think that members of the court simply followed the regulation requiring dismissal, believing that at some point afterward President Arthur or other reviewing authorities would reduce the sentence, as indeed was almost the case.

During the lengthy review process, Flipper remained legally a second lieutenant in the army, and members of the military establishment were choosing sides. Colonel Grierson stated his position almost immediately. Within days, he had personally discussed the case with Captain Barber and then wrote Flipper saying he trusted "that you will come out all right in the end and soon be reinstated to duty."

Grierson also was trying to arrange with General Augur a transfer of Flipper as an "effective means" of removing him "as quickly as possible from unsatisfactory and . . . dangerous surroundings and influences." He threw in a word of advice to Flipper:

> In my judgment you should at once and for *all times cut loose* from all *association* calculated to lead you into trouble. You cannot exercise too much caution and should be sure to conduct yourself as to make it impossible for any one either friends or foes to have it in their power to find just cause to censure you for either official or private conduct for the future.[18]

Was Grierson advising him to "cut loose" from Lucy Smith? Or did he, too, see a conspiracy against Flipper? Possibly he meant both.

Less than two weeks after Flipper's court-martial ended, Shafter resurrected the Berger affair, once again charging Flipper with embezzlement and conduct unbecoming an officer. As departmental judge advocate, Clous opposed the action, because he felt the result would be essentially the same as in the court-martial just held. Nevertheless, General Augur approved the charges and ordered Flipper to trial once more. The new charges were sent to Washington for review together with the trial record and, ultimately, the Judge Advocate General's Office ordered them dropped.[19]

On January 2, 1882, Augur finished his review of the proceedings of Flipper's trial. He disapproved the acquittal on embezzlement, stating that the evidence was sufficient "to fully establish the allegations in the specifications and 'embezzlement' under the 60th Article of War." He approved the conviction for conduct unbecoming an officer, as well as the sentence of dismissal.[20]

Augur's action on the embezzlement charge was not as arbitrary as one might think. At the time, Army Regulations were vague on the matter, and the government had made a case for constructive embezzlement. Augur, therefore, may have believed that the acquittal was erroneous and that Flipper was, in fact, guilty. Once again, however, the wording of the charge applied to actual embezzlement, a case the government had *not* been able to prove. This was noted by Judge Advocate General Swaim, who disallowed, once and for all, the question of embezzlement. In his recommendation to Secretary Lincoln, Swaim wrote, "It is clear that Lieut. Flipper did not intend to defraud the government out of any of its funds but that his conduct is attributable to carelessness and ignorance of correct business methods. I think therefore that the finding of not guilty on the charge of embezzlement is correct and proper."

The conviction for conduct unbecoming an officer and a gentleman would have to stand, but even there, Swaim saw mitigating circumstances. Feeble as it was, Flipper's contention that Shafter was out to get him appeared valid to the judge advocate general, who wrote:

> Subsequent developments convinced Lieut. Flipper that his information concerning the disposition of Shafter was correct. It is believed that there is no case on record in which an officer was treated with such personal harshness and indignity upon the causes and grounds set forth as was Lieut. Flipper by Col. Shafter and the officers who searched his quarters taking his watch and ornaments from him; especially as they must have known all the facts at the time and well knew that there was no real ground for such action.

In view of this, Swaim wrote, "I would recommend the sentence be continued but mitigated to a lesser degree of punishment."[21]

Swaim's conclusions apparently were reached upon a misinterpretation of Sergeant Ross's testimony. As previously noted, Ross said he made out a letter of transmittal on August 10, which Flipper took back to his quarters along with the checks. It was found, still unsigned, together with the checks, when Wilhelmi and Edmunds searched his quarters, the next day. Not until then were any letters of transmittal signed or posted, as Ross made clear in his testimony. Swaim, however, apparently believed that the letter had already been submitted and that Shafter and Wilhelmi "must have had knowledge of the non transmittal of the funds at the time they ransacked Flipper's quarters"—hence, a conspiracy to discredit Flipper. In fact, neither Shafter nor Wilhelmi had ever seen the letter until it was recovered in the search.[22]

Lincoln's observations are not recorded, but probably they were passed on to President Arthur in a verbal discussion of the case. Perhaps they considered the adverse reaction to Arthur's decision earlier that year to throw out the Whittaker conviction; perhaps not.[23] Whether this had a bearing on Arthur's decision in the Flipper case may never be known. There is another possible reason for Arthur's final decision. During the first year of the Civil War, the future president had served as quartermaster general of New York. In a position notorious for graft and corruption, he served impeccably, arranging the rapid deployment of more than two hundred thousand well-equipped troops to the front, and saving the federal government thousands of dollars.[24] It is conceivable that his own experience, and sense of duty and honesty, made Arthur particularly sensitive to potential corruption in the Quartermaster and Commissary Departments, and prejudiced him against Flipper.

One person who might have swayed the president toward leniency is pointedly missing—Captain Barber. As previously noted, Barber had enough influence with Arthur to obtain a recommendation for promotion for himself, the previous year. Certainly he at least would have been able to discuss the matter with the president, had he been so inclined. There is, however, no record that he ever attempted to bring the matter before Arthur, or that Arthur attempted to contact him about it.

On June 14 Arthur sent the record of trial back with a one-sentence note: "The sentence in the foregoing case of Second Lieut. Henry O. Flipper, 10th Regiment of U.S. Cavalry, is hereby confirmed."[25]

There was nothing more to be done. In keeping with Colonel Grierson's request, Flipper had been transferred to Fort Quitman, which was about as far into oblivion as an officer could go. There he spent his last six months as a soldier. Fort Quitman was garrisoned by his own company, but as an officer in arrest, he could not accompany it beyond the boundaries of the post. As his old friend Captain Nolan was on extended leave, the company was under temporary command of Lieutenant Nordstrom. Bored and frustrated and, as Barry Johnson notes, with nothing to do but eat, sleep, and read, Flipper probably "developed to the full" his hatred of Nordstrom during this period.[26]

At noon June 30, 1882, 2nd Lt. Henry Ossian Flipper ceased to be a soldier.[27] There was no ceremony of any kind. The order simply went into effect at the specified time.

12

AFTER THE ARMY

For the first time in his adult life, Henry Flipper was a civilian and had to look after himself. He went to El Paso, where he said he "did nothing special worth mentioning" until the fall of 1883, when he went to work as an assistant engineer for an American company developing mines in Chihuahua.[1] This was the beginning of a long and successful career as a mining engineer throughout the Southwest, Mexico, and South America. He worked both for the federal government and for private companies, and he gained a reputation for his knowledge of mining laws in the various countries of Latin America. Yet throughout this time, he never relented in his determination to be reinstated in the army.

In the nineteenth century, military justice offered no appeal outside army channels. Once these had been exhausted, only an act of Congress, approved by the president, could overturn the sentence of a court-martial. Although Flipper requested a copy of the proceedings from the Adjutant General's Office in Washington almost immediately,[2] he waited sixteen years before initiating his appeal to Congress. He justified the delay by saying that he was "thoroughly humiliated, discouraged, and heart-broken" and that he realized he "was not sufficiently removed from the excitement and prejudices of the time." He also contended he did not have sufficient political or military influence to present his case in what he considered "its true aspect." And finally, he said, "I preferred to go forth into the world and by my subsequent conduct as an honorable man and by my character disprove the charges."[3]

The timing is also significant. When Flipper finally made his appeal, the United States had just declared war on Spain, and he contended he could "apply the training and ability acquired by me at the Military Academy to the service of the government."[4] Earlier in the year, when the prospect of war was still being debated, he wrote the secretary of war offering his services should conflict occur, an offer that was ignored.[5]

Over the ensuing months, Congress was too preoccupied with the war to give any consideration to dismissed former officers. Once the open conflict with Spain ended and the United States found itself suppressing an insurrection in the newly acquired Philippines, Flipper saw another opportunity. He was now known in Washington from an appearance before the Supreme Court in a lengthy land claim case, and he was assisted by Barney McKay, a former sergeant of the black Ninth Cavalry, who had become an influential author and editor.

With McKay's help, bills to reinstate Flipper were introduced in both the Senate and the House of Representatives. They were virtually identical, except the Senate bill authorized back pay and allowances, whereas the House bill did not. Personally, Flipper did not seek any special treatment, only restoration to the service with the grade and rank he would have attained had he not been dismissed.[6]

The bill went before the House Committee on Military Affairs, where Flipper presented his version of what he now considered to be the facts. Among them was this amazing statement:

> When I was relieved from duty as Quartermaster I had no secure place to keep the commissary funds, and so reported to Colonel Shafter. He expressly told me to keep them in my quarters, that they would no doubt be safe there fore a few days until he relieved me and I turned them over to my successor. Colonel Shafter denied all knowledge of the interview ... and, instead of relieving me from duty as Acting Commissary of Subsistence within "a few days," waited until the 10th of August, five months, during which time I kept the commissary funds in my trunk in my quarters with his full knowledge and consent, notwithstanding his denial.[7]

There is no record of such an "interview" or of Shafter's denial because the interview never took place. Flipper's statement to the Committee on Military Affairs is in total contradiction to his own statement to the court, almost two decades earlier, that he had kept the funds in his trunk because he considered it the most secure place. As Clous pointed out to the court, Flipper had access to a large, virtually immobile safe, with a sentry posted to guard it after hours. Shafter had every reason to believe he was using that safe, and the fact that Flipper was storing the money in his trunk probably came as a complete surprise.

Flipper also said that Shafter came up with the idea of submitting the personal check for $1,440.43,[8] an allegation totally unsupported by the evidence. If Shafter had done so, why wasn't it brought out in the trial? Had there been any truth in this, a competent attorney like Merritt Barber would have jumped on it immediately, and Shafter himself very likely would have faced charges.

Upon "discovering" the discrepancy, Flipper said:

I was afraid to consult the commanding officer, or any other officer of the post, because I had heard frequent stories from civilians about the post that the officers there were plotting to get me out of the Army . . . and because I had seen Lieutenant Louis Wilhelmi, Regimental Adjutant of the 1st Infantry and other officers prowling around my quarters at unseemly hours of the night.[9]

Wilhelmi had been dead for more than a decade when this allegation was made, and thus was unable to defend himself. Flipper conveniently neglected to mention that he not only was regimental adjutant of the First Infantry but also post adjutant of Fort Davis. As post adjutant, he was the senior administrative officer of the garrison, and in that capacity it makes perfect sense that Wilhelmi would, from time to time, make night rounds of the post for guard inspection and other purposes. The layout of Fort Davis was such that anyone out for a night stroll along the west side of the parade ground could have been accused of "prowling around" Flipper's quarters—or those of any other officer including Colonel Shafter, for that matter.

As for the "civilians about the post," why were they not summoned to testify during the trial? Several civilians of the community appeared as character witnesses on Flipper's behalf. These were successful, respected businessmen, whose relationship with Fort Davis—as an institution and as a garrison of individual soldiers—was one of interdependence. They needed the army for business, but the army needed them for goods and services. Yet there is not one word in their testimony concerning a conspiracy against Flipper. The only hint of anything out of line was lawyer Dean's warning that Flipper should be careful of Shafter; and that came *after* his arrest, when Flipper still regarded the colonel as "his friend."

To Congress and in his memoirs, Flipper alleged a conspiracy to discredit him, and he named Shafter, Nordstrom, and Wilhelmi as parties to it.[10] In his petition to the Senate, he went so far as to claim Shafter told him to keep the money in his trunk so that Wilhelmi and Nordstrom could steal it. According to Flipper, it would have been easy enough, because he shared a house with Nordstrom.[11]

Again, Flipper was leveling an accusation against an officer who could not defend himself; Nordstrom died earlier in 1898. Aside from that, there are several problems with this statement. Post returns show that Nordstrom was in the field with Company A during much of the time Flipper's troubles were developing. In August, with Flipper already in arrest, he was at Fort Davis, having been ordered to take over Flipper's caseload as judge advocate. On September 28 he left with the company for Fort Quitman, and there he remained.[12] Despite Flipper's allegations in the Quarles letter, Nordstrom was not summoned as a witness during the trial. In fact, his name was never even mentioned in court. Finally, assuming Wilhelmi and Shafter did plan to steal the money and frame Flipper, the planting of evidence in Flipper's room would have required the cooperation of Bates, Edmunds, and Sergeant Ross.[13] Could a plan requiring that many people possibly have been kept so quiet that not a word of it got out to the soldiers on post, or to the ever-alert Barber? And would any of them have trusted Nordstrom, a man notorious for his irrational temper and big mouth?

If Nordstrom had been summoned as a witness, or his name mentioned, Barber would have needed a reason, and the only reason would have been Mollie Dwyer. Yet she, likewise, never was mentioned during the trial, or in Flipper's subsequent petitions. In fact, the only time she appears in the entire affair is in Flipper's private memoir of 1916. Why? Because the implied relationship between Flipper and Mollie never existed. As previously noted, such a relationship would have attracted attention particularly in the isolated, self-contained atmospheres of Fort Sill, Fort Elliott, and Fort Davis. Had the crux of the matter actually been a relationship with Mollie Dwyer, would an attorney of Barber's disposition have let it pass?[14]

One name is scrupulously absent from all Flipper's later allegations—Lucy Smith. Flipper never mentioned her in his subsequent memoirs, or in any of his appeals. It is as though she had ceased to exist. Yet Lucy, of all people, had the most access to the money in Flipper's trunk. In spite of his protestations of caution, the evidence shows he was notoriously casual in letting her go through his things. The search in Shafter's office recovered almost three thousand dollars in cash and checks she had concealed about her body. If anyone stole the money, it was Lucy, either alone or together with any of the other shadowy figures who, testimony revealed, apparently had routine access to Flipper's quarters. As Barry Johnson notes, Flipper could not "publicly admit that the blind trust which he had reposed in his housekeeper, and probable mistress, had been so ruinously betrayed. He probably never admitted this even to himself."[15]

Although Clous brought out that Lucy was under indictment in U.S. district court, the record is vague as to her life after Flipper's trial. No one has ever officially determined what happened to the missing money, and Lucy Smith, one of thousands of rootless wanderers who populated the western frontier, disappears from history.

Had the African American community rallied behind Flipper at this point, there is a chance that Congress might have given him some sort of satisfaction. But aside from Barney McKay, the community as a whole is conspicuous because of its silence. There appears to have been a continuing feeling that Flipper had betrayed a trust. As early as 1877 a chaplain of the Twenty-fifth Infantry noted that black soldiers believed "the colored people of the whole country are more or less affected by their conduct in the Army." The black community did, in fact, look up to its soldiers as symbols of a future in which African Americans as a whole might take their rightful place in society.[16] Thus it might be surmised that troubles involving the army's one black officer might be taken as a setback, particularly when that officer was Henry Flipper, who already had offended black leaders by his elitism.

Flipper could have mended fences. At the time of his dismissal, he still was not yet thirty. Had he been able to put the court-martial behind him, his education and his talents might have placed him on a plane with Booker T. Washington and W. E. B. Du Bois in the nascent civil rights movement. Yet he apparently was not interested in his fellow African Americans unless it suited his purposes, and he likely continued to believe that having served as an *officer* in some way set him above the rank and file of the black community. Even more telling than his early remarks in *The Colored Cadet* is a letter from Flipper to Booker T. Washington, during the effort to get his bill through Congress. Writing of recent racial incidents between black troops and citizens, he commented:

> The disgraceful conduct of the colored volunteers in the south has reduced my chances at least fifty per cent. In Macon, Georgia, a soldier of one of these regiments went into a place of business and asked to be served. He was refused. He went to camp and got about half a hundred of his comrades, came back and undertook to get revenge. Now, in my opinion, this was wholly uncalled for. He was simply inviting trouble instead of trying to avoid it. This statement of the case may not be true, but it is the one published to the country and believed by those to whom we have to look for assistance in such cases as mine. This conduct on the part of the colored volunteers is making the putting of more colored men in the reorganized Army extremely problematical. These soldiers have seemed to think that because they wore the government's uniform they were at liberty to

avenge all the wrongs *they conceive* the white people of the South have ever done to them. [italics added][17]

It was as though Flipper were saying, "How dare these blacks insist on their dignity as human beings and soldiers when my petition is before Congress?" Small wonder, then, that his case drew little response from black leaders.

If Flipper was offended by the conduct of black soldiers insisting on rights, he was not above seeking the support of his supposed enemy, Colonel (now Brigadier General) Shafter. Only two weeks later, he sent another letter to Booker T. Washington. After recapping Shafter's initial mistreatment of him, he added that the colonel's testimony at the trial

was fair and straightforward and he gave me the most excellent character as an officer. [He d]etailed the various theories he had adopted and followed out and frankly stated that they had all ended in nothing. He is a vain man and can be reached through his vanity. I am almost afraid of him. A word from him in this case would have great weight, a word against me would defeat my bill and a word favorable to me would, I believe, just as certainly secure the passage of that measure. If you are well enough acquainted with General Shafter to do so, you might feel him [out] and if he shows a favorable disposition in the matter, you might ask him to aid us. If you catch him in the right humor, *he will consent, I am sure, to aid us.* [italics added][18]

It seems incredible that Flipper would believe that Shafter might help him, considering the allegations in his petition. Washington may have thought so, because there is no indication that he answered this particular letter, or that he ever mentioned to matter to Shafter. Perhaps Washington, too, had had enough of Henry Flipper.

Barber is conspicuously absent from Flipper's efforts for reinstatement, as he had been from the presidential review. It is significant, however, that on June 29, 1882, two weeks after his former tutor, President Arthur, approved the sentence, he was promoted to major and assigned to Washington as assistant adjutant general. By the time of Flipper's 1898 petition, he was a full colonel in the Adjutant General's Office, and thus in a position to be of some assistance. Yet there is no mention of him. Considering his disenchantment with frontier duty, together with his service in two other high-profile trials during the same period as Flipper's, one cannot escape the suspicion, as historian Thomas D. Phillips has suggested, that in handling the Flipper case, Barber was submitting an elaborate application for transfer.[19] As it stands, following his interview with Colonel Grierson at Fort Concho immediately after the trial, Barber disappears from Flipper's life.

Flipper's 1898 petition to Congress brought no results. In all likelihood, the congressional sponsors, once they had thoroughly studied the case, realized they were dealing with something of a red herring and quietly let the matter drop. Several other efforts were made on Flipper's behalf, primarily through the unceasing efforts of Barney McKay.

The bill that probably came closest to succeeding was introduced in 1921. This would have placed Flipper on the retired list with the rank he would have held had he remained in the army—that is, colonel of the cavalry. Reaction was mixed. On the one hand, Brig. Gen. Anson Mills (ret.), the officer who supposedly had canceled the dinner in Flipper's honor at Fort Concho many years before, supported the bill, saying he had always believed Flipper innocent. On the other hand, Secretary of War John W. Weeks flatly opposed it on the grounds that Flipper had been duly dismissed under sentence of court-martial. Senator George W. Pepper, to whom the bill was assigned, agreed with Weeks. Concluding his report, Pepper said, "[T]he whole evidence seems convincing that he deserved what he got."[20]

Pepper's report, written in the summer of 1922, prompted the Senate Committee on Military Affairs to postpone the bill indefinitely. On September 9, however, Secretary of the Interior Albert Fall intervened. Fall, a New Mexico attorney, had become acquainted with Flipper in 1893, when both were involved with the Court of Private Land Claims, in which Flipper acted as special agent for the Department of Justice. From then on, they worked together frequently until, by about 1905, Flipper had become more or less a permanent associate, assisting Fall in various capacities. Now that he was secretary of the interior, Fall wrote Senator James W. Wadsworth, Jr., chairman of the committee, expressing disappointment in the committee's lack of action. In the letter, Fall wrote that, having talked to various officials in West Texas, he had come to this conclusion:

> I think without exception those civilians who know of the Flipper case sympathize most fully with him in his trouble, and this is in a district where the negro has no voice in affairs, and receives but scant courtesy or consideration, as practically all the old time white residents were Southern born and life-long Democrats.

Fall went on to detail all Flipper's accomplishments in the Southwest and Mexico since his dismissal from the army, and concluded by saying:

> The enactment of the bill would simply result in his restoration and immediate retirement on account of age.
>
> Of course I am aware that some of our officers are opposed to the passage of this bill; I have hoped, however, that a thorough consideration by the Committee, and after the Secretary of War had also personally considered the matter, would have resulted favorably.[21]

In deference to Secretary Fall, Wadsworth agreed to consider the bill for resubmission to the committee. Before he could do so, however, the Sixty-seventh Congress expired, and the bill died. It was reintroduced into the new Congress in 1924, but by then Fall had been forced to resign because of his involvement in the Teapot Dome scandal, thus depriving Flipper of his highest-placed supporter. The bill died one last time, and there were no further efforts. Flipper dropped his quest for good.[22]

One might ask if racism was a factor in his failure to obtain reinstatement. The possibility cannot be ignored. Heitman's *Historical Register* contains many cases of white officers who were reinstated after dismissal. Then again, it also contains many instances of white officers who—for whatever reasons— were not reinstated. It is significant that reinstatements generally occurred within a reasonable period of time, such as under ten years, indicating a prompt petition for reinstatement. Such was the case of Flipper's associate at Fort Stockton, Capt. George Armes, who, upon dismissal in 1870, immediately petitioned, and was reinstated in 1878.[23] An immediate petition appears to have crossed Flipper's mind when he requested a copy of the proceedings. The fact remains, however, that he waited. Therefore, if one considers the possibility of racism in the failure to reinstate Flipper, one must also consider the possibility that the sixteen-year wait, together with the allegations against officers now dead and the overall tone of the petition, may have worked against him.

Flipper never married. In 1891 and '92, while living in Arizona, he had a seven-month common-law arrangement with a local woman named Luisa Montoya. Arizona's antimiscegenation law prohibited a formal marriage because Hispanics were legally classified as white, and it is doubtful Flipper would have married anyway because he was contemptuous of western women of any race. In 1918, or perhaps even earlier, he renewed his early relationship with Anna White, now Anna White Shaw, a widow with two grandchildren, to whom he had been engaged during his last year at West Point. Once again, they became engaged, and once again, nothing came of it, this time because Flipper left to work in Venezuela.[24]

Even at this stage, Flipper retained the attitudes and prejudices instilled by his own early experiences, and by his years as an army officer. Despite his dismissal, he was intensely nationalistic, and despite any cordiality toward individual Mexicans, he shared the view that as a people they were essentially inferior. When the *Washington Eagle* accused him of recruiting former black soldiers to join Pancho Villa's revolutionary Army of the North against Brig. Gen. John J. Pershing's Expeditionary Force, he sent a blistering reply expressing complete support for Pershing, and attesting to the loyalty of current and former black troops. While a mining consultant for Albert Fall, he sent reports from the Mexican border that supported Fall's view that the United States should intervene in Mexico.[25] None of this, however, changed his overall status, vis-à-vis the army.

In 1931, alone and essentially penniless, Flipper retired to Atlanta, where he moved in with his brother, Joseph, now a bishop of the African Methodist Episcopal Church. Over the next nine years until his death, he was a recluse, seldom leaving the house. He sat in his room reading Scripture but never spoke of what he had read. He died of a heart attack while dressing for breakfast on May 3, 1940. In the space on the death certificate for occupation, Joseph wrote "Retired Army Officer." His body was placed in a plain wooden coffin and buried without any government marker in Southview Cemetery in Atlanta.[26]

In 1972 Ray O. MacColl, a Georgia schoolteacher, ran across the Flipper affair while studying black cowboys. Feeling an injustice had been done, he contacted U.S. Representative Dawson Mathis, who urged the Department of the Army to reopen the case. A formal application was filed by Flipper's niece, Irsle King, and nephew, Festus Flipper, seeking reversal of the conviction for conduct unbecoming an officer and a gentleman. On November 17, 1976, the Army

Board of Corrections of Military Records convened to examine the case.[27]

Once again, the timing is significant. It was only a few months before the centennial of Flipper's graduation from West Point. Additionally, the army was trying to rehabilitate its image from allegations of promiscuous drafting and expending of African Americans and other minority troops in Vietnam. The board ducked the issue of reversing the conviction by ruling that it did not have the authority to do so. On the other hand, it determined that in view of Flipper's prior service record and the peculiar conditions cited by both Barber and General Swaim, his punishment was excessive. Consequently, Flipper's dismissal was upgraded to an honorable discharge, retroactive to June 30, 1882, the date he left the service.

One must question how thoroughly the board reviewed the record in light of one of the statements in its conclusions: "that the evidence of record tends to show that he may not have been provided with adequate means to properly safeguard the funds."[28] The government's position that Flipper had available "a strong, heavy and secure safe, over which after hours a sentinel stood guard, [and] the regulations of his department required [him] to keep public funds in that safe" appears to have been completely ignored.

The vote of the board was not unanimous, however, with one of the five members dissenting. The dissenting member (who was not identified) stated Flipper's record of false reports and statements "clearly represents misconduct of a very serious nature and should not be taken lightly." The member added that even though Flipper was acquitted of embezzlement, "it appears that he was guilty of misappropriation of some of the funds in question." Because of these factors, the member felt the sentence should be allowed to stand.[29]

That, however, was only one member's opinion. As far as the army now is concerned, Flipper was honorably discharged.

On February 11, 1978, Flipper's remains were exhumed in Atlanta and transferred to Thomasville, Georgia, where Mayor J. A. Bracy proclaimed "Henry Ossian Flipper Day." The following day, a memorial service was held at the First Missionary Baptist Church. Georgia governor George Busbee issued a proclamation commending Flipper "for his many years of service to his country." A burial detail from Fort Benning then loaded the coffin onto a gun carriage, which was drawn to Old Magnolia Cemetery to a grave site next to his parents. Lieutenant Henry Flipper was reinterred as a soldier with full military honors.[30]

While Flipper was responsible for his own problems, one cannot ignore the impact his case must have had on the army's view of African Americans as officers. In his history of black troops on the Texas border, James Leiker discounts a racist conspiracy to evict Flipper from the army but does point out that black soldiers served on a perpetually probationary status. Offenses by white soldiers were seen as individual character flaws, but the same offenses by African Americans were presumed to be representative of an entire race. Flipper, then, would have been subjected to double scrutiny. As an officer, he was expected to maintain a higher standard of conduct than other soldiers of any race. He also was essentially the test cases of whether a black man could maintain that standard. In committing the unacceptable offense of lying to his military superiors, he betrayed the standard and, by extension, severely hampered any opportunity for black soldiers to rise within the ranks.[31] Given the paucity of African American officers into the twentieth century, this conclusion is difficult to refute. The Flipper affair itself was not an example of "institutionalized racism," but it undoubtedly reaffirmed the stereotypes and hindered the chances of black soldiers to receive commissions. Merritt Barber was correct when he told the court that Flipper's success or failure would weigh on the future of African Americans as officers.

In successfully completing the program at West Point, and receiving his commission, Flipper did much to advance the cause of equality in the army. In throwing it all away, he set the cause into slow motion, and it took decades to recover. In the end, his brief military career did more harm than good.

NOTES

ABBREVIATIONS

AAG	Acting Adjutant General
AG	Adjutant General
AJAG	Acting Judge Advocate General
DT	Department of Texas
JAG	Judge Advocate General
USA	United States Army

PREFACE

1. Robinson, "Court-Martial," 20–25.

2. The National Archives has further compounded the problem for researchers in its arrangement of this microfilm, which is available to the public. For whatever reason, the seemingly complete 1898 petition was placed at the very *beginning* of the reel, so Flipper's version of the affair is the first thing the researcher sees. All other material in the file is arranged in chronological order.

3. *Flipper's Dismissal* was published in a limited printing of 150 numbered and three unnumbered copies and is now extremely difficult to obtain. I acquired one of the unnumbered copies through

the kindness of Barry Johnson in 1991. At the time, he advised me that he understood an American dealer was buying virtually every copy that came on the market in order to control the availability.

4. Barry Johnson to the author, November 6, 1992.

5. The Drew case is discussed in Love, *One Blood*.

INTRODUCTION

1. Billington, *New Mexico's Buffalo Soldiers*, 190; Foner, *Blacks and the Military*, 64–65. Alexander was commissioned as a second lieutenant in the Ninth Cavalry, a position he held at the time of his death in 1894. Young was posted to the Tenth Cavalry upon graduation. Although he was assigned to the Seventh Cavalry in December 1896, he was transferred to the Ninth Cavalry a little over nine months later and spent the rest of his career in black Regular or Volunteer units. See U.S. Congress, House, *Historical Register and Dictionary of the United States Army, From Its Organization, September 29, 1789, to March 2, 1903*, by Francis B. Heitman (hereafter cited as Heitman, *Historical Register*), 1:156, 1066.

2. Kinevan, *Frontier Cavalryman*, 305n40. Kinevan, a graduate of West Point and the University of California–Berkeley School of Law, at various times represented both the government and the defense in courts-martial, as well as serving as trial judge, appellate defense counsel, and military court of review judge.

3. Tuchman, *March of Folly*, 46.

4. Petition for Pardon, 18, in "To Right a Past Wrong," Fort Davis National Historic Site.

5. The petition for clemency called the dismissal "the equivalent of a modern dishonorable discharge" (ibid., 16). In fact, the equivalent of a modern dishonorable discharge was known as "cashiering," which was under dishonorable circumstances and did stigmatize the soldier in question. Heitman, *Historical Register*, makes the distinction between officers dismissed from the service and officers who were cashiered.

6. Whittaker's case is described in detail in Marszalek, *Court-Martial*, and Marszalek, "Black Cadet."

7. Marszalek, "Black Cadet," 106.

8. Smith, *U.S. Army*, 46–47.

9. These forms are among the documents submitted as evidence by the government and are included in National Archives Microfilm Publication T-1027. This extensive microfilm collection contains the bulk of the War Department's record relating to Flipper (hereafter cited as Flipper File).

10. *Globe*, September 24, 1881. The letter will be discussed in Chap. 4.

11. Clinton, "Remarks by the President."

12. Dobak and Phillips, *Black Regulars*, 202.

13. Williams, *Texas' Last Frontier*, 169–71. Thus far, there has been no serious study of the Fort Stockton incident. Williams shrugs it off as essentially anecdotal, basing much of his account on Bliss's memoirs. Citing the "scientific ignorance" of the medical profession at the time, he appears almost to accept Bliss's view that Taylor believed he had been "hoodooed" and died of fright. Certainly the belief in conjuring a person to death existed in black communities at the time, and to some extent it still exists, particularly in Louisiana. Nevertheless, the Army Medical Corps of the 1870s was not as primitive as is generally believed. Competent army surgeons had a reasonably good understanding of both combat trauma and various other soldier ailments. Often they were more innovative and farsighted than their civilian counterparts in treatment, use of disinfectants, and emphasis on sanitation, proper diet, and uncontaminated drinking water. See Rickey, *Forty Miles a Day*, 130–33, and Sohn, *Saw*, 82–89.

14. William H. Leckie, telephone conversation with the author, June 2002.

15. Of the seven presidents from U. S. Grant in 1869 through William McKinley in 1901, only Grover Cleveland did not have some sort of Union army service record.

16. Johnson, *Flipper's Dismissal*, 50; Knight, *Life and Manners*, 72–73. *General Courts-Martial* lists all officers tried by general court-martial during the period 1809–90. In the summer of 2003, I compiled the names of those tried during the three years 1880–82 and compared it with their service records as given in Heitman, *Historical Register*, vol. 1. Among the officers dismissed from service under sentence of court-martial (and these are few), there is only the slightest discrepancy between those with Union army service and those without. Nevertheless, in specific cases, particularly those involving public funds and veracity of an officer's word, a Civil War record appears to have been a mitigating factor.

17. Heitman, *Historical Register*, 1:821.

18. Johnson, *Flipper's Dismissal*, 87–88.

19. Heitman, *Historical Register*, 1:938. Near the end of the Civil War, many people were breveted for "faithful and meritorious service" as an acknowledgment of distinguished service in whatever capacity. A brevet promotion for "gallant and meritorious service," however, indicated valor in action.

20. U.S. Department of War, OAG, *General Court-Martial Orders, 1881.*

1. RACE AND THE ARMY

1. Binkin et al., *Blacks and the Military*, 12; Wesley and Romero, *Afro-Americans in the Civil War*, 55–57; Cornish, *Sable Arm*, 15.

2. Wesley and Romero, *Afro-Americans in the Civil War*, 101.

3. Cornish, *Sable Arm*, 15; Foote, *Civil War*, 3:859–60; Jones, *Rebel War Clerk's Diary*, 2:415. The Confederate government could authorize formation of black units but could not itself offer emancipation. This would have entailed depriving owners of their property, something the general government had no authority to do. Consequently, the government could only advocate that individual states use their authority to emancipate African Americans in exchange for military service.

4. Cornish, *Sable Arm*, 10–11. When Maj. Gen. John Charles Frémont published an order in 1861 that included freeing slaves held by Southern supporters in Missouri, Lincoln forced him to rescind that portion of the order, on the basis that the sole purpose of the war was preservation of the Union. Lincoln's action raised a storm of public protest in abolitionist circles. Ibid., 12–14.

5. Ibid., 12–13, 17–24.

6. Ibid., 29–30.

7. Ibid., 51–52.

8. Ibid., 29–30; Binkin et al., *Blacks and the Military*, 13; Glatthaar, *Forged in Battle*, 31–32; Catton, *This Hallowed Ground*, 222.

9. Wesley and Romero, *Afro-Americans in the Civil War*, 38–39.

10. Ibid., 67.

11. Ibid., 103.

12. Glatthaar, *Forged in Battle*, 201–206.

13. Taylor, introduction to *Buffalo Soldier Regiment*, by John H. Nankivell, ix; Billington, *New Mexico's Buffalo Soldiers*, 3.

14. Billington, *New Mexico's Buffalo Soldiers*, 3–4; Leckie, *Buffalo Soldiers*, 6.

15. Leckie, *Buffalo Soldiers*, 6. In 1869 a general reduction of the army amalgamated the four black infantry regiments into two.

16. Ibid., 6–7.

17. Ibid., 13–14.

18. Wedemeyer, "Memoirs," 2:99; Smith, *Dose of Frontier Soldiering*, 41.

nistrative position, in the nineteenth century it held substan-
udicial responsibilities. As for the rides Flipper mentioned in
nemoirs, one must conclude that if they did occur, they
ubtedly would have been during officers' outings and picnics,
lar activities both at Fort Sill and at Fort Davis, rather than the
e intimate situations Flipper attempted to convey.

7. In *Black Frontiersman* (161–62n6), the updated edition of
o *Frontiersman*, editor Theodore D. Harris comments that Flip-
association with Mollie Dwyer was "the cause of malicious
.p at Fort Sill and later at Forts Elliot and Davis," but does not
ide a source for that information.

8. Flipper, *Negro Frontiersman*, 19–20. Johnson (*Flipper's Dis-
al*, 64–65) points out that Nordstrom, sixteen years older than
er, was a self-educated man. While apparently honest and
r, he nevertheless had a foul disposition, which brought him an
iordinary number of courts-martial during his career. For his
Flipper tended to view uneducated or self-educated people—
k or white—as his social inferiors. His 1916 diatribe against
lstrom was accompanied by the comment that most of the
r officers at Fort Davis were "hyenas." This, however, contra-
an observation by Colonel Grierson, who, upon assuming com-
d of Fort Davis in 1882, noted that most of the officers of the
h Cavalry on post were unhappy over Flipper's dismissal from
ervice. See Taylor, introduction to *Colored Cadet*, xvii; Leckie
Leckie, *Unlikely Warriors*, 280.

9. Dobak and Phillips, *Black Regulars*, 64, 189; Johnson, *Flip-
Dismissal*, 64–65; Taylor, introduction to *Colored Cadet*, xvii;
man, *Historical Register*, 1:750; Flipper, *Negro Frontiersman*,

10. Charles Berger to Lt. Charles Nordstrom, December 28,
l, with endorsement, Flipper File.

11. Presidio County, Statement of Louis Duval, quartermaster
>n master, Fort Davis, February 18, 1881; Proceedings of a Board
irvey convened at Fort Davis, Texas, pursuant to the following
r: Headquarters, Fort Davis, Texas, February 17, 1881, Orders
31, all in Flipper File.

12. Bvt. Maj. Gen. Samuel Holabird, Acting Quarter Master
eral USA, to AAG DT, August 19, 1881, with eighth endorse-
t by Capt. J. W. Clous, AJAG DT, December 21, 1881, ibid.

13. Flipper, *Negro Frontiersman*, 19.

14. Fowler, *Black Infantry in the West*, 26.

15. Shafter's life and career are covered by Paul H. Carlson,
:os Bill": A Military Biography of William R. Shafter*, and

19. Foner, *Blacks and the Military*, 59–61; Dobak and Phillips,
Black Regulars, xvi–xvii; Glatthaar, *Forged in Battle*, 202; Taylor,
introduction to *Buffalo Soldier Regiment*, x, and *Racial Frontier*,
Chap. 6; Leiker, *Racial Borders*, 14–15, Chap. 5; Utley, "'Pecos Bill'
on the Texas Frontier," 6.

20. Leckie, *Buffalo Soldiers*, 6–7; Glatthaar, *Forged in Battle*,
Chap. 6; quote from McConnell, *Five Years a Cavalryman*, 213.

21. Leckie, *Buffalo Soldiers*, 6.

22. Leiker, *Racial Borders*, 77.

23. Quoted in Foner, *Blacks and the Military*, 65, and in Fowler,
Black Infantry in the West, 135; see also Schofield, *Forty-six Years
in the Army*, xx, 445–46. Schofield refers specifically to a scandal
involving the beating of another black cadet, Johnson Whittaker,
who arrived three years after Flipper. Nevertheless, his account
sums up the attitude of many of the era's senior officers toward
African Americans as a race.

2. THE BLACK CADET

1. Flipper, *Colored Cadet*, 7; Carroll, *Black Military Experience*,
347.

2. Owens, *This Species of Property*, 177–80.

3. Flipper, *Colored Cadet*, 8–9. As they were themselves chat-
tels, slaves could not legally own property or receive money in their
own names; it all had to belong to their master. By "protection,"
Henry Flipper meant that if someone tried to cheat a slave, Ponder
could intervene on the slave's behalf on the grounds that legally he,
and not the slave, was being cheated.

4. Ibid., 7–11; Taylor, introduction to *Colored Cadet* (1998
reprint), x.

5. Flipper, *Colored Cadet*, 11–13; Taylor, introduction to *Colored Cadet*, xi–xii.

6. Litwack, *Been in the Storm So Long*, 513, 541–42. In *Black
Culture and Black Consciousness* (285–89), Lawrence W. Levine
notes the touchiness over degrees of color that appears to have per-
meated black society well into the twentieth century. He speculates
that the prejudices of white American society were so ingrained that
they were absorbed by black people, to the extent that they classified themselves and each other according to a multitude of shades.
He also points out, however, that the animosity was mutual
between persons of lighter and darker shades.

7. Flipper, *Colored Cadet*, 11–13.

8. Carroll, *Black Military Experience*, 264; Foner, *Reconstruction*, 423–24.

9. Flipper, *Colored Cadet*, 18–19; Thomas Powell, M.D., statement of physical condition of Henry O. Flipper, April 2, 1873; J. A. Holtzclaw to J. C. Freeman, April 3, 1873; Freeman to Secretary of War, April 8, 1873; Flipper to Secretary of War, April 17, 1873, all in U.S. Department of War, "Records Relating to the Army Career of Henry Ossian Flipper, 1873–1883," National Archives Microfilm Publication T-1027. This extensive microfilm collection contains the bulk of the War Department's record relating to Flipper (hereafter cited as Flipper File).

10. Black and Black, *Officer and a Gentleman*, 61n.

11. Flipper, *Colored Cadet*, 29, 312–13.

12. Ibid., 292; Carroll, *Black Military Experience*, 264–65.

13. Flipper, *Colored Cadet*, 37n.

14. Ibid., 13–14, 30, 42.

15. Taylor, introduction to *Colored Cadet*, xvii–xviii.

16. Flipper, *Colored Cadet*, 179–81.

17. Taylor, introduction to *Colored Cadet*, xvii–xviii; Flipper, *Colored Cadet*, 282. Besides remarking on those he considered "unadulterated" (i.e., pure African), Flipper noted that Smith "was rather light, possibly an octoroon." Ibid., 288.

18. Flipper, *Colored Cadet*, 14, 36, 143–44; Black and Black, *Officer and a Gentleman*, 71; Atkinson, *Long Gray Line*, 62.

19. Flipper, *Colored Cadet*, 280–82; Marszalek, *Court-Martial*, 39–40.

20. Flipper, *Colored Cadet*, 244–45, 255–56; Carroll, *Black Military Experience*, 348–49; Flipper to E. D. Townsend, AG USA, July 23, 1877, Flipper File.

21. Taylor, introduction to *Colored Cadet*, xxii.

22. Flipper, *Colored Cadet*, 112.

23. Ibid., 276; Flipper, *Negro Frontiersman*, 2, 5.

24. *Negro Frontiersman*, edited by Theodore D. Harris and published posthumously by Texas Western Press in 1963, was reprinted by Texas Christian University Press in 1997, under the title *Black Frontiersman*. The original edition was the only one available at the time of my initial writing of *The Court-Martial of Lieutenant Henry Flipper*, and for the sake of conformity, it is used for this volume as well.

25. Nolan's background is discussed in Altshuler, *Cavalry Yellow and Infantry Blue*, 246–47.

26. Nicholas Nolan to Robert Newton Price, September 4, 1879, abstracted in Grierson Papers, Military Correspondence.

27. Nicholas Nolan to Robert Newton Pri[ce] 1879, Grierson Papers, Military Correspondence.

28. Flipper, *Negro Frontiersman*, 2–3. Accord Nolan family insisted that he board with them, wh their meals. This is plausible; hospitality among families was common, and there was nothing un bining resources and sharing meals. Even if Flippe lar at the Nolan table, it is reasonable to presum invited over from time to time. See Knight, *Life a*

29. Flipper, *Negro Frontiersman*, 8. Flipper e Mills "a native born Texan." He was from Indi spent much of his civilian life in Texas and clain dence. Likewise, he refers to Tear as "McTear" of t Infantry. Heitman, *Historical Register*, lists no off of "McTear" but notes (1:950) a Wallace Tear of Infantry. Both the Twenty-fourth and Twenty-fifth ments, units of which were posted to Fort Concho

30. Flipper, *Negro Frontiersman*, 16; Leckie, 224–29; Grierson to Whom It Concerns, November File.

3. Links in a Chain

1. The commissary office standing today on t Fort Davis National Historic Site came into use afte ture, and therefore it is not the one under discussi The history of Fort Davis is described in several wor *Fort Davis National Historic Site, Texas* by Robe *Fort Davis: Outpost on the Texas Frontier* and *Fron Fort Davis and the West*, both by Robert Wooster.

2. Flipper, *Negro Frontiersman*, 16–18. Flip received these positions as a sort of reward for his field. In fact, as Lt. Col. Thomas T. Smith, former a sor of military history at West Point, notes, these "usually the lot of very junior officers." Smith, *Dose diering*, 197n4.

3. D. G. Swaim, JAG USA, to Robert Todd Linco War, March 3, 1882, Flipper File.

4. Flipper, *Negro Frontiersman*, 2–3.

5. Myers, *Westering Women*, 85–86.

6. Texas laws concerning black-white sexual rel cussed in Robinson (no relation to the author), "Leg Although in modern times the Texas county judgesh

Robert M. Utley, "'Pecos Bill' on the Texas Frontier." See also Smith, *Dose of Frontier Soldiering*, 40 (quote), 198n5.

16. In his diary for that week, Capt. William George Wedemeyer noted Shafter's progress toward Fort Davis saying, "Col. Shafter with headquarters of 1st Infantry arrive by the stage road and camp about a mile above my camp [Camp Charlotte, forty-two miles from Fort Concho]. Mrs. Shafter is with him and so is Lt. Wilhelm [*sic*], his adjutant, and Lt. Strother, quarter master." Wedemeyer, "Memoirs," 2:110. This shows Shafter intended from the outset to fill the two appointive positions with his own people.

17. Record of Trial, 53–54, Flipper File.

18. Carlson, *"Pecos Bill,"* 122; Flipper, *Negro Frontiersman*, 20; Dinges, "Henry O. Flipper," 13; U.S. Senate, Committee on Military Affairs, 12–13, Flipper File; U.S. Department of War, Returns of U.S. Military Posts, Fort Davis, January, March 1881; Heitman, *Historical Register*, 1:933, 1036. Carlson notes that Shafter's action may have been racially motivated, but he also points out that these staff changes were "fairly standard" practice. In *The Court-Martial of Lieutenant Henry Flipper*, I wrote that Wilhelmi replaced Nordstrom as adjutant. In fact, the Fort Davis post returns for January 1881 state that Nordstrom had been relieved by McFarland two months earlier. It should be noted that Wilhelmi had served under Shafter as regimental adjutant of the First Infantry since March 16, 1880, and Strother, as quartermaster since August 18, 1880.

19. Dinges, "Henry O. Flipper," 14; Swaim to Lincoln, March 3, 1882, Flipper File.

20. Swaim to Lincoln, March 3, 1882, Flipper File. The irregular visits of the paymaster often left soldiers without cash, and therefore unable to pay either their commissary bills or their laundry bills. The inability to collect meant that laundresses also ran up substantial bills with the commissary department. See Wooster, *Frontier Crossroads*, 82–83.

21. Michael Small to ACS (Flipper), Fort Davis, June 29, 1881, Flipper File.

22. Swaim to Lincoln, March 3, 1882, ibid.

23. Committee on Military Affairs, 13–14, ibid. One must again question Flipper's veracity. The $1,440.43 necessary to cover the check would be in excess of $15,000 in today's currency. Even in the twenty-first century, a royalty of this amount is extremely rare, except for the best selling of authors. Flipper was hardly an established author, and his publisher, Homer Lee & Co. was, as Barber acknowledged (Record of Trial, 193, ibid.), a contract printer specializing in banknotes. The $74 that Flipper actually received from

Homer Lee & Co. seems more within what should have been his expectations.

24. Shafter to AAG DT, August 13, 1881; Shafter to Small, August 10, 1881; Swaim to Lincoln, March 3, 1882, all in Flipper File.

25. Shafter to AAG DT, August 13, 1881, ibid.

26. Shafter to Small, August 10, 1881, ibid.

27. Swaim to Lincoln, March 3, 1882; Shafter to AAG DT, August 13, 1881; Testimony of Lt. Louis Wilhelmi, Record of Trial, 203, all in Flipper File; Dinges, "Henry O. Flipper," 15. The details of Shafter's reprimand, his observation of Flipper's horse at Sender and Siebenborn's, his subsequent accusation of Flipper, and the reluctance of Wilhelmi and Edmunds to conduct a search are discussed in a letter to the *Dubuque Daily Herald*, by Capt. Kinzie Bates's wife, Lillie, which was published on August 25, 1881. She indicated that Bates also was involved in the search and determined the cinders found in the fireplace were not destroyed checks. The letter was reprinted in the *St. Louis Daily Globe-Democrat*, September 2, 1881. An unattributed clipping also is filed in the William R. Shafter Collection, Folder 76, Stanford University.

28. Lillie Jennings Bates, *Dubuque Daily Herald*, August 25, 1881.

29. *United States of America* v. *Lucy Smith*, statements by Lucy E. Smith and William R. Shafter, August 22, 1881; Shafter to AAG DT, August 13, 1881, both Flipper File.

30. Shafter to AAG DT, August 13, 1881, ibid. The arbitrariness and pettiness of this action toward an officer become all the more apparent when one considers Post Surgeon Harry E. Brown's dissatisfaction with the guardhouse, expressed only five weeks prior to Flipper's incarceration. In his monthly report for June, Brown stated the prison rooms needed to be larger, and Shafter's endorsement totally agreed. However, the colonel noted that lack of funds prevented construction of a more adequate guardhouse for the time being. This means Shafter was completely aware that he was imposing undue hardship by incarcerating Flipper. A new guardhouse was erected the following year. Sanitary Report of Post, rendered by Surgeon H. E. Brown, U.S. Army, Post Surgeon, June 30, 1881, endorsement by William R. Shafter, June 30, 1881, U.S. Department of War, Medical History of Fort Davis, Texas.

31. Swaim to Lincoln, March 3, 1882, Flipper File.

32. Thomas Vincent, AAG DT, to Commanding Officer [Shafter], Fort Davis, August 16, 1881, ibid.

33. Record of Trial, 111–12, ibid.

34. R. C. Drum, AG USA, to Brig. Gen. C. C. Augur, August 23, 1881, ibid.

35. Shafter to Vincent, August 16, 1881; Swaim to Lincoln, March 3, 1882, both in ibid.; *Globe*, September 24, 1881.

36. Shafter to Vincent, August 17, 1881, Flipper File.

37. Shafter to AAG DT, August 29, 1881; Frank Edmunds to Small, September 3, 1881, both in ibid.

38. Swaim to Lincoln, March 3, 1882, ibid. The complete charges and specifications are in the Record of Trial, 36–42, ibid.

39. U.S. Department of War, *Regulations of the Army of the United States*, Article 76, para. 1577, states specifically: "Every person having moneys of the United States in his hands or possession who fails to deposit them according to law and the instructions of the proper authority, shall be deemed guilty of embezzlement and punished as provided by law" (176).

40. Ibid., para. 1583:

Every disbursing officer of the United States who deposits any public money intrusted to him in any place or in any manner, except as authorized by law, or converts to his own use in any way whatever, or loans with or without interest, or for any purpose not prescribed by law withdraws from the Treasurer or any Assistant Treasurer or any authorized depository, for any purpose not prescribed by law transfers or applies any portion of the public money intrusted to him, is, in every such act, deemed guilty of an embezzlement of the money so deposited, converted, loaned, withdrawn, transferred, or applied; and shall be punished by imprisonment with hard labor for a term not less than one year nor more than ten years, or by a fine of not more than the amount embezzled or less than one thousand dollars, or by both such fine and imprisonment. (177–78)

41. Record of Trial, 36, Flipper File.

42. Thomas D. Phillips to the author, August 31, 2002.

43. Committee on Military Affairs, 23, 28, Flipper File.

44. Smith, *View from Officers' Row*, 6.

45. Grierson to Alice Kirk Grierson, August 19, 1881, Grierson Papers.

46. *Nation*, September 1, 1881.

47. Ibid., September 29, 1881, October 6, 1881.

48. San Antonio *Daily Express*, September 7, 1881.

49. OJAG, *U.S. Army General Courts-Martial* (hereafter cited as *General Courts-Martial*), 16:1877–83 QQ; Grierson to Alice Kirk Grierson, September 15, 1881, Grierson Papers. Spencer was convicted and dismissed from the service. He had been dismissed under

sentence of court-martial once before, in 1875, but was reinstated two years later. See Heitman, *Historical Register*, 1:911.

4. THE COURT-MARTIAL BEGINS

1. Headquarters, Department of Texas, Special Orders No. 108, September 3, 1881, Record of Trial, 1–2, Flipper File.

2. Carlson, *"Pecos Bill,"* 78–79; see also Leckie and Leckie, *Unlikely Warriors*. Shafter ordered Nolan court-martialed for lack of vigorous pursuit of Indians following Nolan's destruction of a hostile camp and stores in 1875. Grierson intervened, and Nolan got off with a reprimand. Although neither Carlson nor William and Shirley Leckie, in their biography of the Griersons, specifically mention a feud between the two men, all indicate their relations were not cordial beyond what was required by their positions. Carlson goes so far as to call Grierson "Shafter's old nemesis" (133).

3. Grierson to Alice Kirk Grierson, September 6, 1881, Grierson Papers.

4. Augur to Grierson, September 5, 1881, RG 393, Letters Sent by Headquarters Department of Texas, 1870–1894 and 1897–1898 (hereafter cited as Letters Sent).

5. Grierson to Augur, September 6, 1881, Grierson Papers.

6. Augur to Grierson, September 6, 1881, Letters Sent.

7. Johnson, *Flipper's Dismissal*, 50; Utley, *Frontier Regulars*, 85.

8. Johnson, *Flipper's Dismissal*, 50–51; Knight, *Life and Manners*, 71–73.

9. Heitman, *Historical Register*, 1:782–83, 876; Johnson, *Flipper's Dismissal*, 51–52.

10. Wedemeyer, "Memoirs," August 26, 1881, 132; Smith, *Dose of Frontier Soldiering*, 41.

11. Heitman, *Historical Register*, 1:520, 963, 995; Johnson, *Flipper's Dismissal*, 52.

12. *General Courts-Martial*, 16:1877–83 QQ. The case concerned Lt. F. L. Davies, Twenty-second Infantry, who was sentenced to dismissal.

13. In 1886 Clous was appointed to the Judge Advocate General's Office and to the professorship of law at West Point. On My 22, 1901, two days before his retirement, he was appointed brigadier general and judge advocate general. Johnson, *Flipper's Dismissal*, 53; Heitman, *Historical Register*, 1:311–12.

14. Committee on Military Affairs, 22–23, Flipper File; Flipper, *Negro Frontiersman*, 41.

15. Johnson, *Flipper's Dismissal*, 54; Record of Trial, 27, Flipper File.

16. Johnson, *Flipper's Dismissal*, 53–54. When the Articles of War were replaced by the Uniform Code of Military Justice, following World War II, the judge advocate's role became that of a prosecutor. Although these changes were made to dilute the arbitrary nature of military justice and bring it more into line with civilian judicial proceedings, there are those in the military who question whether the system actually has benefited.

17. Flipper, *Colored Cadet*, 73–74; Taylor, introduction to *Colored Cadet*, xxx; *General Courts-Martial*, 16:1877–83 QQ; Thomas Vincent, AAG DT, to Commanding Officer, Fort Davis, August 15, 1881 (two telegrams), Letters Sent. Bates also had served on the Spencer court-martial board.

18. Record of Trial, 3, 6, Flipper File.

19. Ibid., 6–7.

20. In *A Treatise on Military Law and the Jurisdiction, Constitution, and Procedure of Military Courts*, published in 1879, Lt. Rollin Ives, Fifth Artillery, assistant professor of law at West Point, wrote, "The accused is entitled to counsel upon his trial as a *right*. . . . Any person of good standing, civil or military, may be admitted to act as counsel" (105).

A year later, however, Maj. William Winthrop, judge advocate, Bureau of Military Justice, contradicted this by writing, "[I]n general it is to be said that the admission of counsel for the accused in military cases, is not a right but a privilege only, but a privilege almost invariably acceded and as a matter of course; and the whether the counsel proposed to be introduced be military or civil, or a professional or unprofessional person." Winthrop, *Military Law and Precedents*, 165.

21. Quarles died of pneumonia in Flushing, New York, on January 28, 1885, at the age of thirty-eight. *Brooklyn Daily Eagle*, January 29, 1885; Flipper, *Colored Cadet*, 270–71.

22. This section is taken from the *Globe*, September 24, 1881, which printed the entire letter, and from extracts printed in the *Nation*, September 29, 1881,, the *People's Advocate* (a black weekly journal published in Washington), October 1, 1881,, and the *San Antonio Daily Express*, October 4, 1881. It also was printed in the *New York Evening Post*, September 29, 1881, and the *Army and Navy Journal*, October 1, 1881.

23. *Globe*, September 24, 1881; *People's Advocate*, October 1, 1881.

24. Record of Trial, 417, Flipper File.

25. Flipper, *Negro Frontiersman*, 40–41.

26. *General Courts-Martial*, 16:1877–83 QQ; Wedemeyer, "Memoirs," August 25, 1881, 2:131–32. The Spencer trial was controversial in that the officers of the First Infantry at Fort Stockton appear to have closed ranks around Spencer in order to "make a slight attempt to manufacture public opinion," notwithstanding that he was a cavalry officer. See Wedemeyer, "Memoirs," August 24, 1881, 2:131–32.

27. Vincent to Flipper, October 10, 1881, Letters Sent; Grierson to Flipper, October 25, 1881, Grierson Papers.

28. Barber's being appointed to these panels was highly unusual. Normally, court-martial boards consisted of officers from within the defendant's own department, or at the very least from the division of which that department was a part (in Whittaker's case, the Military Division of the Atlantic). Barber, however, was one of several members of the Whittaker board who were serving in either the Military Division of the Missouri or the Military Division of the Pacific, anywhere from one thousand to three thousand miles from New York. This may have been at the behest of Brig. Gen. O. O. Howard, soon to become superintendent of West Point, who suggested to then-President Rutherford B. Hayes that non–West Pointers make up the majority of the board to avoid academy bias as much as possible. Barber was not a West Pointer. See Marszalek, *Court-Martial*, 153, 163–65.

29. Sullivan, *Fort McKavett*, 47, 52, 54. Fort McKavett was ordered to be completely abandoned as of July 31, 1882. Because of the large quantity of stores and equipment, however, this was not feasible, so the post was occupied for an additional eleven months.

30. Wedemeyer, "Memoirs," undated [January 1881], 2:100.

31. Ibid., February 2, 1882, 2:155; Heitman, *Historical Register*, 1:190; Johnson, *Flipper's Dismissal*, 52–53; In —Memoriam: Merritt Barber. The Barber-Arthur connection is not mentioned by Thomas C. Reeves in his biography of Arthur, *Gentleman Boss*, but this does not preclude its existence. The Flipper and Whittaker cases likewise are not discussed, as they probably would have been mere historical footnotes in the overall record of Arthur's life and administration.

32. G. B Russell, Aide-de-camp, DT, to Barber, September 24, 1881; Vincent to Flipper, October 10, 1881; Vincent to Barber, October 10, 1881, all in Letters Sent.

33. Flipper, *Negro Frontiersman*, 41.

34. Record of Trial, 8–13, 19–20; Exhibit 3, 636, both in Flipper File; quotes from Augur to AG USA, October 13, 1881, Letters Sent.

35. Exhibit 2, 633–35, Flipper File.
36. Record of Trial, 14–19, ibid.
37. Ibid., 20.
38. Holabird to AAG DT, August 19, 1881, with endorsement by Clous, December 21, 1881; Flipper File.
39. Record of Trial, 22–24, ibid.
40. Ibid., 24–30.
41. Ibid., 30.
42. Ibid., 30–31.
43. Ibid., 31.
44. Ibid., 31–32.
45. Ibid., 32–33.

5. SHAFTER ON THE DEFENSIVE

1. Record of Trial, 35–42, Flipper File.
2. Ibid., 42–43.
3. Ibid., 44–46.
4. Ibid., 46–49.
5. Ibid., 40–51.
6. Ibid., 51–52.
7. Ibid., 52–53.
8. Ibid., 53–54.
9. Ibid., 55.
10. Ibid., 56.
11. *San Antonio Daily Express*, November 5, 1881.
12. Record of Trial, 66, Flipper File.
13. Ibid., 68–69.
14. Ibid., 69–72.
15. Lucy Smith's status at Fort Davis is at best vague. She appears to have been just as she was represented, a household servant who almost certainly saw to Flipper's sexual interests as well. Had she been a laundress, she would have been classified as "military personnel," with certain specified legal rights, and Shafter could not have arbitrarily ordered her off post. The positions of laundress and household servant are discussed in Stallard, *Glittering Misery*, Chap. 3.
16. Record of Trial, 76–77, Flipper File.
17. Ibid., 77–78.
18. Ibid., 82.
19. Carlson, *"Pecos Bill,"* 195.
20. Record of Trial, 82–83, Flipper File.
21. Ibid., 84.

22. Ibid., 85–88.

23. Ibid., 92–93.

24. Ibid., 94.

25. Ibid., 96–97.

26. *San Antonio Daily Express*, November 8, 1881.

27. Record of Trial, 104–108, Flipper File. Clous apparently suffered from migraines because this was the first of several times his headaches interrupted the proceedings. They no doubt were aggravated by the constant hammering from Barber, much of which was over matters that were trivial at best. It is significant that whenever he asked for a recess, Colonel Pennypacker was more than happy to accommodate. This leads to speculation that, considering his overall state of health, Pennypacker was anxious for any excuse to rest. He retired on disability in July 1883, less than two years after the Flipper trial.

28. Ibid., 108–10.

29. Ibid., 99–100.

30. Ibid., 101.

31. Ibid., 101–102.

6. A Question of Persecution and a "Mexican Theory"

1. Record of Trial, 104–108, Flipper File.

2. Ibid., 114–15.

3. Ibid., 115–16.

4. Ibid., 117.

5. Ibid., 126.

6. Ibid., 183–84.

7. Ibid., 190–91.

8. Ibid., 192–94.

9. Ibid., 196–98.

10. Ibid., 198–99.

11. Ibid., 207–208.

12. Ibid.

13. Ibid., 217–20.

14. Ibid., 220–21.

15. Johnson, *Flipper's Dismissal*, 63–65.

16. Record of Trial, 239, Flipper File.

17. Ibid., 240.

18. Ibid., 260–61.

19. Ibid., 262.

20. Ibid., 263.

21. Ibid., 264–65.

22. Ibid., 266.
23. Ibid., 267, 275–76.
24. Ibid., 284–85.
25. Ibid., 287–90.
26. Ibid., 300–303.
27. Ibid., 303–304.
28. Ibid., 307.

7. The Government Rests

1. Record of Trial, 316, Flipper File.
2. Ibid., 317.
3. Ibid., 326.
4. Flipper to Post Adjutant [Wilhelmi], Fort Davis, August 17, 1881, Exhibit 90, 729, Flipper File; introduced as evidence, Record of Trial, 329, ibid.
5. Johnson, *Flipper's Dismissal*, 62.
6. Record of Trial, 330, Flipper File.
7. Ibid., 331–33.
8. Ibid., 336.
9. Ibid., 381–82.
10. Ibid., 383–84.
11. Ibid., 379, 384.
12. Ibid., 383; Johnson, *Flipper's Dismissal*, 67.
13. Record of Trial, 339, Flipper File.
14. Ibid., 352.
15. Ibid., 362–64.
16. Ibid., 390.
17. Ibid., 396.
18. Ibid., 393–94.
19. Ibid., 394.
20. Ibid., 416–17.

8. Lucy Smith Testifies

1. *San Antonio Daily Express*, November 30, 1881; Record of Trial, 439–40, Flipper File.
2. Record of Trial, 20–21, 424–25, Flipper File. The Whitman saddle was an experimental pattern issued to some cavalry units for field trials beginning in 1879. By 1885 it had fallen out of favor, in part because of the vast stocks of McClellan saddles that remained on hand in ordnance depots. The government-issue saddlebags for the Whitman were the California type, mounted on a stud immediately

behind the cantle, with straps from either side of the saddle inserted through staples on the bags. A six-foot strap, passed under the horse, further steadied the bags. Because of the design of the saddle, Flipper's custom bags would have been attached in a similar fashion. See Steffan, *United States Military Saddles*, 94–98.

3. Record of Trial., 427–28, Flipper File.

4. Ibid., 432.

5. Ibid., 433.

6. Ibid., 436–37.

7. Ibid., 441.

8. Ibid., 320–21.

9. Ibid., 78.

10. Ibid., 449.

11. Knight, *Life and Manners*, 4, 6; Wooster, *Frontier Cross-roads*, 83–84. One government historian has speculated that this relationship, rather than race or anything supposedly involving Mollie Dwyer, was Flipper's undoing:

> At this point I can't prove my theory that [Shafter] was not strongly prejudiced against Flipper for being black but was most upset when he came to Fort Davis and found that Flipper was engaged in activities that violated the code (the other officers were upset too). Just what these violations were is difficult to tell. They probably involved sex. There wasn't much around Fort Davis that Flipper could get. He could not very well have an affair with the visiting single female relatives that stayed with the other officers; families—the white batchelors [*sic*] could, of course. I'd guess that he took in the black "cook" and lived with her too openly for the stomachs of the "colonel's ladies".

Erwin Thompson to Superintendent Frank Smith, Fort Davis, and Mary Williams, Fort Davis, November 18, 1970, Henry Ossian Flipper Files, Fort Davis National Historic Site.

12. Record of Trial, 457, Flipper File.

13. Ibid., 444–45.

14. Ibid., 445–46.

15. Ibid., 446–48.

16. Ibid., 449.

17. Ibid., 450.

18. Ibid., 454.

19. Ibid., 456–57.

20. Ibid., 462.

21. Ibid., 462–63.

9. Testimonials to a Good Name

1. *San Antonio Daily Express*, December 6, 1881.
2. Ives, *Treatise on Military Law*, 314, 316.
3. Record of Trial, 478–79, Flipper File.
4. Ibid., 480–81.
5. Ibid., 481.
6. Ibid., 484.
7. Ibid., 485–86.
8. Leckie and Leckie, *Unlikely Warriors*, 275; Carlson, "*Pecos Bill*," 125–26.
9. Record of Trial, 487–90, Flipper File.
10. Ibid., 490; Ives, *Treatise on Military Law*, 314.
11. Record of Trial, 493, Flipper File.
12. Grierson to Whom It Concerns, November 1, 1881, Flipper File.
13. Record of Trial, 494–96, ibid.
14. Ibid., 496–501.

10. The Question: Can an Officer Be Black?

1. Record of Trial, 503–506, Flipper File.
2. Ibid., 509–11.
3. Ibid., 524.
4. Ibid., 525.
5. Ibid., 530.
6. Ibid., 532–33.
7. Ibid., 535–37.
8. Ibid., 539.
9. Johnson, *Flipper's Dismissal*, 50.
10. Record of Trial, 557–61, Flipper File.
11. Ibid., 572–75.
12. Ibid., 576.
13. Ibid., 578.

11. The End of a Career

1. Record of Trial, 585–86, Flipper File.
2. Ibid., 587.
3. Johnson, *Flipper's Dismissal*, 50.
4. Record of Trial, 585, Flipper File.
5. Ibid., 587.
6. Ibid., 588.

7. Ibid., 600–601.

8. Ibid., 604.

9. Ibid.

10. Ibid., 605.

11. Johnson, *Flipper's Dismissal*, 81.

12. Flipper to Armes, January 9, 1881, extract in Armes, *Ups and Downs*, 509. Although a capable combat officer, Armes had his share of run-ins with the military establishment as well. He had been dismissed from the service under sentence of court-martial in 1870 (Heitman, *Historical Register*, 1:169, says honorably discharged) but was restored to rank in 1878. Almost immediately, however, he crossed with Major McLaughlin, the post commander, and from there, his career again went downhill, until ultimately he faced another court-martial. Although Armes was white, he, like Flipper, considered himself the target of a conspiracy by the "bootlicker" Grierson, and various others, including the "Dutchman" Clous, who served as judge advocate at his trial at Fort Stockton in 1880. At the time of Flipper's letter, Armes was serving out a sentence of suspension and confinement to post. He details his problems at length in *Ups and Downs of an Army Officer*.

13. Johnson, *Flipper's Dismissal*, 81.

14. Record of Trial, 613, Flipper File.

15. More typical was the Spencer court-martial, which organized on August 24 and closed on September 5. By the end of the following day, the board also had tried several enlisted men. Wedemeyer, "Memoirs," 2:131–33.

16. Kinevan, *Frontier Cavalryman*, 304–305n38.

17. Swaim to Lincoln, March 3, 1882, Flipper File.

18. Grierson to Flipper, December 13, 1881, Grierson, Documents and Letters.

19. Clous to Augur, December 21, 1881, with endorsement, Flipper File; Swaim to AG USA, March 10, 1882, Flipper File.

20. Record of Trial, 606, ibid.

21. Swaim to Lincoln, March 3, 1882, ibid. Normally, Swaim would have forwarded his recommendations to Sherman. Since the latter was absent from Washington, the recommendations went directly to Secretary Lincoln.

22. Record of Trial, 394; Swaim to Lincoln, March 3, 1882, both in Flipper File; Johnson, *Flipper's Dismissal*, 84–86.

23. The Whittaker case brought calls in the Senate for investigation of the West Point program and caused a rift between the executive branch and civilian administration of the War Department on the one hand and the army command on the other. The president of

e Military in American History: A New
Praeger Publishers, 1974.

ar: A Narrative. Vol. 3, *Red River to*
: Random House, 1974.

Infantry in the West, 1869–1891. 1971.
ersity of Oklahoma Press, 1996.

l in Battle: The Civil War Alliance of
hite Officers. Baton Rouge: Louisiana
1990. Reprinted 2000.

Booker T. Washington Papers. Vol. 4.
linois Press, 1975.

arber, Colonel, U.S. Army (Retired),
Volunteers." New York: Military Order
the United States, Headquarters Com-
New York. June 15, 1906.

Military Law and the Jurisdiction, Con-
e of Military Courts, with a Summary of
s Applicable to Such Courts. New York:

Dismissal: The Ruin of Lt. Henry O. Flip-
ured Graduate of West Point. London:

Clerk's Diary at the Confederate States
eprint. Alexandria, Va.: Time-Life Books,

r Cavalryman: Lieutenant John Bigelow
iers in Texas. El Paso: Texas Western

anners in the Frontier Army. Norman:
ia Press, 1978. Reprinted 1993.

ffalo Soldiers: A Narrative of the Negro
Norman: University of Oklahoma Press,

irley A. Leckie. *The Buffalo Soldiers: A*
Cavalry in the West. Rev. ed. Norman:
ia Press, 2003.

: General Benjamin Grierson and His
niversity of Oklahoma Press, 1984.

Borders: Black Soldiers along the Rio
on: Texas A&M University Press, 2002.

the court-martial board, Brig. Gen. Nelson A. Miles, was under substantial pressure from his military superiors to make certain Whittaker was discredited. See Marszalek, "Black Cadet," 35–36, and
Wooster, *Nelson A. Miles*, 131–32.

24. Arthur's Civil War service is discussed in Reeves, *Gentleman Boss*, Chap. 2.

25. Arthur, endorsement to Record of Trial, June 14, 1882,
unnumbered page immediately following 606, Flipper File.

26. Johnson, *Flipper's Dismissal*, 92.

27. Headquarters, USA, Office of the Adjutant General, General Court-Martial Orders No. 30, June 17, 1882, Flipper File.

12. AFTER THE ARMY

1. Flipper, *Negro Frontiersman*, 21. In the interim, Flipper
worked as a clerk in a steam laundry. See Taylor, introduction to
Colored Cadet, xxxiii.

2. Flipper to AG USA, December 10, 1881, Flipper File.

3. Committee on Military Affairs, 50–51, ibid.

4. Ibid., 51.

5. Flipper to Secretary of War, February 14, 1898, quoted in
Johnson, *Flipper's Dismissal*, 94; Flipper, *Negro Frontiersman*, 39.

6. Flipper, *Negro Frontiersman*, 38–39; Johnson, *Flipper's Dismissal*, 94–95; 55th Cong., 2nd sess., H.R. 9849, Flipper File.

7. Committee on Military Affairs, 12, Flipper File.

8. Ibid., 13–14.

9. Ibid., 15–16.

10. Flipper, *Negro Frontiersman*, 20.

11. Johnson, *Flipper's Dismissal*, 65–66.

12. Post Returns, Fort Davis, Texas, May–December 1881.
Nordstrom was in the field May 3–21, and again beginning May 30.
In August he was listed as present at Fort Davis with his company,
but by then Flipper's problems had already surfaced.

13. Carlson, *"Pecos Bill,"* 126.

14. One could argue that in the social climate of the 1880s, Barber and Flipper would not have "compromised" a lady by bringing
her name up in court. Such gallantry was fodder for the contemporary French romantic novelist Ouida, who wrote of young men sac-
rificing themselves on the altar of chivalry to preserve the fame of a
lady. In reality, though, and with his career on the line, would Flipper have hesitated, particularly if he already had flaunted the iron-
clad prohibitions against interracial relations? Nordstrom and

Government Documents

Clinton, William Jefferson. "Remarks by the President at Ceremony in Honor of Lt. Henry O. Flipper." Washington, D.C.: United States Department of State International Information Programs, February 19, 1999.

U.S. Congress, House. *Historical Register and Dictionary of the United States Army, From Its Organization, September 29, 1789, to March 2, 1903*, by Francis B. Heitman. 2 vols. 57th Cong., 2nd sess., H. Doc. 446. Washington, D.C.: Government Printing Office, 1903.

U.S. Department of War. Letters Sent by Headquarters Department of Texas, 1870–1894 and 1897–1898. National Archives Microfilm Publication 1114 Roll 6. RG 393. Washington, D.C.: National Archives and Records Administration, n.d.

———. Medical History of Fort Davis, Texas. Electrostatic copy. Fort Davis National Historic Site.

———. Office of the Judge Advocate General (OJAG). *Register of the Records for the Proceedings of the U.S. Army General Courts-Martial 1809–1890*, vol. 16, 1877–83 QQ. National Archives Microfilm Publication M1105 Roll 7. Washington, D.C.: National Archives and Records Administration, n.d.

———. Office of the Adjutant General (OAG). *General Court-Martial Orders, Adjutant General's Office, 1881.* Washington, D.C.: Government Printing Office, 1882.

———. "Records Relating to the Army Career of Henry Ossian Flipper, 1873–1883." National Archives Microfilm Publication T-1027. Washington, D.C.: National Archives and Records Administration, n.d.

———. *Regulations of the Army of the United States and General Orders in Force February 17, 1881.* Washington, D.C.: Government Printing Office, 1881.

———. Returns of U.S. Military Posts. Fort Davis, Texas. National Archives Microfilm Publication M617 Roll 985. RG 94. Washington, D.C.: National Archives and Records Administration, n.d.

Winthrop, William. *Military Law and Precedents.* 2nd ed. Originally published in 1880 as *Digest of Opinions of the Judge Advocate General.* Washington, D.C.: Government Printing Office, 1920.

Foner, Jack D. *Blacks an[…] Perspective.* New Y[…]

Foote, Shelby. *The Civ[…] Appomattox.* New […]

Fowler, Arlen L. *The Bl[…] Reprint, Norman: U[…]

Glatthaar, Joseph T. *Fo[…] Black Soldiers and […] State University Pr[…]

Harlan, Louis R., ed. *[…] Urbana: University […]

"In Memoriam: Merri[…] Brigadier-General, U[…] of the Loyal Legion […] mandery of the Sta[…]

Ives, Rollin A. *A Treatis[…] stitution, and Proce[…] the Rules of Eviden[…] D. Van Nostrand, 1[…]

Johnson, Barry C. *Flippe[…] per, U.S.A., First G[…] N.p., 1980.

Jones, John B. *A Rebel W[…] Capital.* Vol. 2. 186[…] 1981.

Kinevan, Marcos E. *Fro[…] with the Buffalo […] Press, 1998.

Knight, Oliver. *Life an[…] University of Okla[…]

Leckie, William H. *The[…] Cavalry in the We[…] 1967.

Leckie, William H., an[…] *Narrative of the B[…]* University of Okla[…]

———. *Unlikely War[…] Family.* Norman[…] Reprinted 1998.

Leiker, James N. *Rac[…] Grande.* College S[…]

Levine, Lawrence W. *Black Culture and Black Consciousness: Afro-American Folk Thought from Slavery to Freedom*. New York: Oxford University Press, 1977.

Litwack, Leon F. *Been in the Storm So Long: The Aftermath of Slavery*. New York: Alfred A. Knopf, 1980.

Love, Spencie. *One Blood: The Death and Resurrection of Charles R. Drew*. Chapel Hill: University of North Carolina Press, 1996.

Marszalek, John F., Jr. "A Black Cadet at West Point." *American Heritage* 22, no. 5 (August 1971): 30–37, 104–106.

———. *Court-Martial: A Black Man in America*. New York: Charles Scribner's Sons, 1972.

McConnell, H. H. *Five Years a Cavalryman*. Jacksboro, Tex.: J. N. Rogers and Co., 1889.

Myers, Sandra L. *Westering Women and the Frontier Experience, 1800–1915*. Albuquerque: University of New Mexico Press, 1982. Reprinted 1999.

Owens, Leslie Howard. *This Species of Property: Slave Life and Culture in the Old South*. New York: Oxford University Press, 1976.

Reeves, Thomas C. *Gentleman Boss: The Life and Times of Chester Alan Arthur*. 1975. Reprint, Newton, Conn.: American Political Biography Press, 2002.

"Re-Interment of Lt. Henry Ossian Flipper." Thomasville, Ga.: First Missionary Baptist Church, n.d.

Rickey, Don, Jr. *Forty Miles a Day on Beans and Hay: The Enlisted Soldier Fighting the Indian Wars*. Norman: University of Oklahoma Press, 1963. Reprinted 1985.

Robinson, Charles F., II, "Legislated Love in the Lone Star State: Texas and Miscegenation." *Southwestern Historical Quarterly* 107, no. 1 (July 2004): 65–86.

Robinson, Charles M., III. "The Court-Martial of Henry Flipper." *True West* 36, no. 6 (June 1989): 20–25.

———. *The Court-Martial of Lieutenant Henry Flipper*. El Paso: Texas Western Press, 1994.

Schofield, John M. *Forty-six Years in the Army*. 1897. Reprint. Norman: University of Oklahoma Press, 1998.

Smith, Sherry L. *The View from Officers' Row: Army Perceptions of Western Indians*. Tucson: University of Arizona Press, 1990.

Smith, Thomas T. *A Dose of Frontier Soldiering: The Memoirs of Corporal E. A. Bode, Frontier Regular Infantry, 1877–1882*. Lincoln: University of Nebraska Press, 1994. Reprinted 1999.

———. *The U.S. Army and the Texas Frontier Economy, 1845–1900.* College Station: Texas A&M University Press, 1999.

Sohn, Anton Paul. *A Saw, Pocket Instruments, and Two Ounces of Whiskey: Frontier Military Medicine in the Great Basin.* Spokane: Arthur H. Clark Company, 1998.

Stallard, Patricia Y. *Glittering Misery: Dependents of the Indian Fighting Army.* Fort Collins, Colo.: Old Army Press, 1978.

Steffan, Randy. *United States Military Saddles, 1812–1943.* Norman: University of Oklahoma Press, 1973.

Sullivan, Jerry M. *Fort McKavett: A Texas Frontier Post.* Lubbock: West Texas Museum Association, 1981.

Taylor, Quintard, Jr. *In Search of the Racial Frontier: African Americans in the American West, 1528–1990.* New York: W. W. Norton and Co., 1998.

———. Introduction to *The Colored Cadet at West Point: Autobiography of Lieut. Henry Ossian Flipper, U.S.A., First Graduate of Color from the U.S. Military Academy,* by Henry O. Flipper. 1878. Reprint, Lincoln: University of Nebraska Press, 1998.

———. Introduction to *Buffalo Soldier Regiment: History of the Twenty-fifth United States Infantry, 1869–1926,* by John H. Nankivell. Lincoln: University of Nebraska Press, 2001.

Tuchman, Barbara W. *The March of Folly: From Troy to Vietnam.* New York: Alfred A. Knopf, 1984.

Utley, Robert M. *Fort Davis National Historic Site, Texas.* National Park Service Historical Handbook Series 38. Washington, D.C.: Government Printing Office, 1965.

———. *Frontier Regulars: The United States Army and the Indian, 1866–1891.* 1973. Reprint, Lincoln: University of Nebraska Press, 1984.

———. "'Pecos Bill' on the Texas Frontier." *American West* 6, no. 1 (January 1969): 4–13, 61–62.

Wesley, Charles H., and Patricia W. Romero. *Afro-Americans in the Civil War: From Slavery to Citizenship.* Cornwell Heights, Pa.: Publishers Agency, 1978.

Williams, Clayton W. *Texas' Last Frontier: Fort Stockton and the Trans-Pecos, 1861–1895.* College Station: Texas A&M University Press, 1982.

Wooster, Robert. *Fort Davis: Outpost on the Texas Frontier.* Austin: Texas State Historical Association, 1994.

———. *Frontier Crossroads: Fort Davis and the West.* College Station: Texas A&M University Press, 2006.

———. *Nelson A. Miles and the Twilight of the Frontier Army.* Lincoln: University of Nebraska Press, 1993.

NEWSPAPERS AND PAMPHLETS

Atlanta Journal and Constitution
Brooklyn Daily Eagle
(Dubuque, Iowa) *Daily Herald*
(New York) *Globe*
Nation
(Washington, D.C.) *People's Advocate*
St. Louis Daily Globe-Democrat
San Antonio Daily Express
Thomasville (Ga.) *Times Enterprise*